BRIEF POINTS

B R I E F
P O I N T S

AN ALMANAC FOR
PARENTS AND
FRIENDS OF
U.S. NAVAL ACADEMY
MIDSHIPMEN

SECOND EDITION

ROSS MACKENZIE

NAVAL INSTITUTE PRESS
ANNAPOLIS, MARYLAND

Library of Congress Cataloging-in-Publication Data

Mackenzie, Ross, 1941–
    Brief Points: an almanac for parents and friends of U.S. Naval Academy midshipmen / Ross Mackenzie. — 2nd ed.
        p.   cm.
    Includes index.
    ISBN 1-55750-584-5 (alk. paper)
    1. United States Naval Academy.   I. Title.
V415.P1M33   1996
359'.0071'173—dc20   96-11801

Printed in the United States of America on acid-free paper   ∞

02 01 00   9 8 7 6 5 4

Unless otherwise noted, all photos, charts, and maps courtesy
U.S. Naval Academy.

CONTENTS

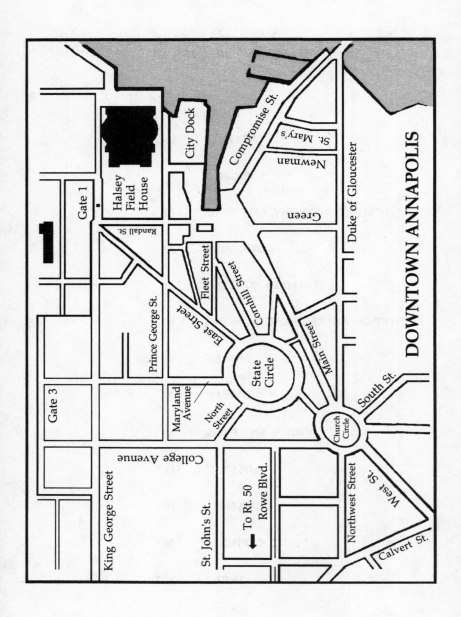

DOWNTOWN ANNAPOLIS

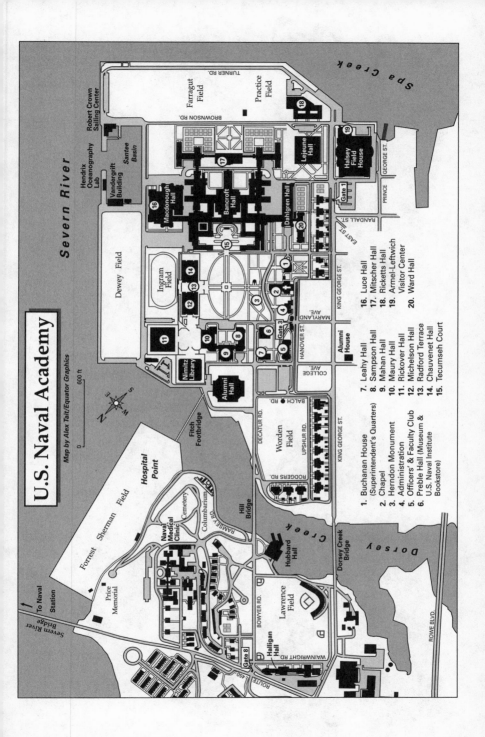

U.S. Naval Academy

Map by Alex Tait/Equator Graphics

Severn River

Spa Creek

Dorsey Creek

To Naval Station

Severn River Bridge

0   600 ft

Hospital Point

Forrest Sherman Field

Price Memorial

Cemetery

Columbarium

Naval Medical Clinic

RAMSEY RD.

Fitch Footbridge

Hill Bridge

Halligan Hall

Gate 8

ROUTE 450

WAINWRIGHT RD.

BOWYER RD.

Lawrence Field

Hubbard Hall

Dorsey Creek Bridge

ROWE BLVD.

KING GEORGE ST.

Worden Field

DECATUR RD.

RODGERS RD.

UPSHUR RD.

BALCH RD.

Alumni Hall

Nimitz Library

COLLEGE AVE.

Alumni House

HANOVER ST.

Gate 3

MARYLAND AVE.

Dewey Field

Ingram Field

Macdonough Hall

Vandergrift Building

Santee Basin

Hendrix Oceanography Lab

Robert Crown Sailing Center

Bancroft Hall

Dahlgren Hall

EAST ST.

RANDALL ST.

Gate 1

KING GEORGE ST.

PRINCE GEORGE ST.

Farragut Field

TURNER RD.

BROWNSON RD.

Practice Field

Lejeune Hall

Halsey Field House

1. Buchanan House (Superintendent's Quarters)
2. Chapel
3. Herndon Monument
4. Administration
5. Officers' & Faculty Club
6. Preble Hall (Museum & U.S. Naval Institute Bookstore)
7. Leahy Hall
8. Sampson Hall
9. Mahan Hall
10. Maury Hall
11. Rickover Hall
12. Michelson Hall
13. Radford Terrace
14. Chauvenet Hall
15. Tecumseh Court
16. Luce Hall
17. Mitscher Hall
18. Ricketts Hall
19. Armel-Leftwich Visitor Center
20. Ward Hall

⚓ ⚓ ⚓ ⚓ ⚓ ⚓ ⚓ ⚓

PREFACE

Want the gouge? You hold it in your hand.

Midshipmen might call this a gouge book [see glossary]. By that they would mean the skinny, the essential information, the fundamental facts. In truth, this is an almanac for family and friends and anyone who wants to tune in to midshipmen. It's a one-step, user-friendly source for all you might ever want (or need) to know about the Naval Academy—or about the four-year cruise there on which a midshipman perhaps close to you is embarked. In terms of scope and detail, nothing approaching this book exists.

Midshipmen at the Naval Academy are *in* the Navy—they're holders of warrants in the naval service. The Academy is the Navy's college. A Superintendent calls the Academy "one of the premier colleges in the world"; the Dean calls it the world's "most highly selective university." It probably is those things. One fact: According to recent data compiled by *USA Today,* the Academy had the lowest average acceptance rate of any institution of higher learning in the United States. It ranks among the top colleges anywhere.

It is also very tough; what's more, its requirement of a major distinguishes it dramatically from even America's other military academies. And in seeking to educate and train midshipmen "morally, mentally, and physically" not only for the Navy and the Marines but for life, it offers an experience vastly different from that offered by any of the nation's civilian colleges—and that is largely because it holds midshipmen to much higher standards.

Those regarding the Naval Academy as a glory experience are usually viewing it from the outside. As the parents of two Academy graduates, my wife and I well know the Academy's regimen: intense, intensive, structured, stressful, demanding, and relentless. The Naval Academy is a crucible, and it certainly is not for everybody. On top of its heavy academics (140 credit hours required for graduation) and its weighty athletics and physical-training (PT) load, it piles approximately 45 semester hours of military/professional courses and—during the four academic years—approximately 2,000 hours of military/professional training. In addition, Bancroft Hall—the heart of Academy life—is a decidedly military atmosphere.

Those sorting through their academic and military obligations in this highly competitive environment spend a good deal of time and energy sorting out themselves as well. They learn the true meaning of self-doubt and self-esteem; along the way they also learn about senior/subordinate relations and how to make the system work for them. Upon graduation, they usually emerge as motivated, confident, mature leaders—morally, intellectually, and physically fit. Quality officers, quality individuals—and no longer steeped (as they were when they entered) in adolescent unreality.

As parents, we also know that the many positives of the Naval Academy outweigh its negatives. Yet this is an age of a widening gap between military and civilian life. Many of the several thousand midshipmen attending the Naval Academy may yearn sometimes, even often, while there for something else in the society we have become. So they require all the understanding and encouragement those who love and support them can give.

That's where this book comes in. It's a guide. A handbook. A manual for family and friends—and others: faculty, staff, sponsors, even midshipmen themselves.

You will find few prideful adjectives here, and little editorializing. Rather, you will find a great deal of information—and usually straight up. *Brief Points,* whose title purposely shadows the Plebe (or freshman) manual called *Reef Points,* is less concerned with philosophy than with facts—less with whys than whats. Not even those new Plebes most familiar with the Academy before they entered understand what the experience is really like. Possibly, even probably, no one can understand until he or she has been aboard a while.

But if anything can help, this book will—containing as it does the gouge on just about every aspect of the Naval Academy today.

BRIEF POINTS

1 / PROFILE

Who are these midshipmen? What are they like? Where do they come from? Where do they go?

On Induction Day, they must be at least 17 and not older than 22. Their high-school and pre-admission records show midshipmen to be by and large hard-working, high-achieving, persevering young men and women. About 80 percent of those entering from high school stand academically in the top 20 percent of their graduating class. They arrive bristling with academic, athletic, extracurricular, and noncurricular awards. More than most of their peers, they are disciplined and focused—and driven, in the words of James Webb's novel about the Academy, by a sense of honor.

During their years in the Academy's never-changing, ever-changing environment, they will know common suffering in a harsh regimen. They will come to hate drill and to dread the Dark Ages. Yet they will emerge vastly more mature than when they entered—steeped in learning and leadership and professionalism, and with an uncommon esprit.

Some statistical pictures of midshipmen, drawn in averages from data about recent classes, look like this....

GEOGRAPHY
In the five classes 1994–1998, these were the *average* numbers of Plebes entering the Brigade from:

Alabama	49	Montana	20
Alaska	11	Nebraska	22
Arizona	55	Nevada	19
Arkansas	24	New Hampshire	27
California	434	New Jersey	195
Colorado	52	New Mexico	26
Connecticut	58	New York	276
Delaware	16	North Carolina	92
District of Columbia	11	North Dakota	16
Florida	242	Ohio	169
Georgia	112	Oklahoma	38
Hawaii	17	Oregon	44
Idaho	17	Pennsylvania	267
Illinois	125	Rhode Island	24
Indiana	66	South Carolina	58
Iowa	38	South Dakota	11
Kansas	29	Tennessee	56
Kentucky	44	Texas	265
Louisiana	41	Utah	16
Maine	27	Vermont	9
Maryland	261	Virginia	255
Massachusetts	91	Washington	82
Michigan	123	West Virginia	28
Minnesota	56	Wisconsin	70
Mississippi	34	Wyoming	17
Missouri	63		

In addition, each year about 12 Plebes entered from U.S. territories, as well as about 39 from 20 foreign countries.

ADMISSIONS
Because of diminishing government appropriations for defense, the Academy is shrinking—along with just about every aspect of the

military. The average size of the Academy's student body—the Brigade—is about 4,000. Yet again (except where noted) using five-year *averages* for the classes 1995–1999, these are the numbers:

—Total applicants: 11,428
—Total applicants with nomination: 5,200
—Total applicants found fully qualified academically, medically, and physically: 1,956
—Total offers of admission: 1,475
—Total admitted: 1,185

—Those taking the SAT:
  Percent entering with SATs 700–800:
    Verbal: 4
    Math: 33
  Percent entering with SATs 600–699:
    Verbal: 32
    Math: 53
  Percent entering with SATs 500–599:
    Verbal: 48
    Math: 13
—Those taking the ACT:
  Percent entering with ACTs 30–36:
    Verbal: 6
    Math: 55
  Percent entering with ACTS 25–29:
    Verbal: 46
    Math: 41
  Percent entering with ACTs 20–24:
    Verbal: 45
    Math: 4

—Those entering from college or with post–high school preparation: 369
—Those entering with at least six months of college: 86
—Those entering from private preparatory schools (no extra year): 76

—Those entering from the Naval Academy Preparatory
 School: 209
—Those entering directly from the fleet (the Navy and
 Marines): 78
—Those entering via the Naval Academy Foundation: 81

—Average number of African Americans entering: 86
—Average number of Asian Americans entering: 47
—Average number of Hispanic Americans entering: 79
—Average number of Native Americans entering: 12
—Average number of minorities (total) entering: 222
—Average number of women entering: 173
—Average number of alumni children entering: 40

GRADUATION
Averages for the classes 1991–1995:

—Average total graduating: 954
  Men: 862
  Women: 92
—Average total of minorities graduating: 162
    African Americans: 51 (including 6 women)
    Asian Americans: 46 (including 6 women)
    Hispanic Americans: 57 (including 5 women)
    Native Americans: 8 (including 0 women)
—Average total retention (attrition): 74 percent (26 percent)
—Average total graduating with distinction: 100

CAREER CHOICES
Averages for the classes 1991–1995:

—Commissioned in the Navy (total): 866
  Men: 780
  Women: 86
—Commissioned in the Marines (total): 139
  Men: 133
  Women: 6

—Navy:

Surface Warfare:
Men: 263
Women: 27

Special Operations:
Men: 8
Women: 1

Special Warfare:
Men: 15
Women (not open to women): 0

Aviation:
Pilot:
Men: 186
Women: 12

Naval Flight Officer (NFO):
Men: 91
Women: 5

Nuclear:
Submarine:
Men: 115
Women (not open to women): 0

Surface:
Men: 40
Women: 2

Staff:
Supply Corps:
Men: 23
Women: 10

Construction Engineering Corps:
Men: 6
Women: 6

Intelligence:
Men: 4
Women: 3

Cryptology:
Men: 2
Women: 1

Aviation Maintenance:
  Men: 0
  Women: 1
Oceanography:
  Men: 2
  Women: 1
Non-Warfare:
  Medical Corps:
    Men: 13
    Women: 1
  Inter-Service Transfer:
    Men: 7
    Women: 1
—Marines:
Ground:
  Men: 92
  Women: 6
Aviation:
  Pilot:
    Men: 36
    Women (open to women class of 1994): 1
  Naval Flight Officer (NFO):
    Men: 5
    Women (open to women class of 1994): 0

MISCELLANEOUS

In its history, the Academy has inducted about 85,000 and commissioned about 63,000 (including about 1,300 women)—a 73-percent retention rate, not far from the 74 percent of recent years (the four-year graduation rate for all U.S. colleges is well below 50 percent). Of those commissioned, about 87 percent have gone into the Navy, 8 percent into the Marines, 3 percent into the Air Force, and less than 1 percent into the Army. Of the Academy's graduates, 77 have won the Medal of Honor and about 40 have become astronauts.

Today, of the 4,500 new officers entering the Navy each year, the Naval Academy provides about 17 percent. The Reserve Officer

Training Corps (ROTC) provides about 23 percent, Officer Candidate School (OCS) about 16 percent, and miscellaneous sources the rest. Retention and promotion rates for Academy graduates are considerably stronger—as much as four times—than for those commissioned from other sources. And far higher percentages of Academy graduates remain on active duty beyond their service obligation, notably for 20 years or more. Academy graduates constitute about 17 percent of total active-duty officers in the Navy (excluding the Marines); of those at flag rank, about half are Academy graduates.

⚓ ⚓ ⚓ ⚓ ⚓ ⚓ ⚓ ⚓ ⚓

2 / HISTORY, ACADEMY, AND YARD

Formation of a naval school defied the efforts of many before Secretary of the Navy George Bancroft, also a distinguished historian, succeeded in 1845. Today Bancroft Hall bears his name.

The Academy's campus, called The Yard, began as fewer than 10 acres populated by 50 midshipmen and seven faculty—plus a Superintendent; today, as a consequence of periodic acquisitions and reclamations, it comprises 338 acres populated by about 4,000 midshipmen and about 600 faculty—plus numerous staff and several hundred support and maintenance personnel. It has top-of-the-line resources for academics, athletics, and military training. The Academy's annual operating budget runs to more than $100 million—including $23 million for The Yard alone—and its annual capital budget to more than $13 million; those are federal outlays, which are variously supplemented by private funds.

Annually, more than 1.5 million tourists visit the Academy and The Yard—declared by the federal government to be a National Historic Site. It is located on the west bank of the Severn River in Annapolis—33 miles east of Washington and 30 miles south of Baltimore.

Since the 1909 demolition of old Fort Severn, which preceded the Naval Academy on its present site (principally about where Bancroft Hall's fifth wing now stands), only two buildings from the Academy's early period remain—the brick guardhouses just inside Gate 3. The smaller building (closer to the Officers' Club) dates from 1881, and the larger dates from 1876.

Also of interest: Next to Gate 3 is a smaller gate known as Bilger's Gate. In the past, midshipmen separating from the Academy often left through it; today few midshipmen use Bilger's Gate (they use the street instead), fearing superstitiously that to do so might cause them to "bilge out"—that is, to separate as well. And to the Bilger's Gate superstition, add these two: (1) No midshipman may pass through Bancroft's main entrance connecting the Rotunda and T-Court. (2) Among the many admonitions affecting Plebes: They are denied the privilege of sitting on benches in The Yard.

The Academy has a broad variety of structures and notable sites [see the maps at the beginning of the book; for hours, see Facilities on page 98]. They range from a 12-meter NASA dish installed on Hospital Point in 1988 and used by various departments to communicate with stationary and quasi-stationary orbiting satellites, to a 490-yard, 13-obstacle obstacle course on Forrest Sherman Field, to a 6,217-yard golf course across the Severn River (and therefore not on The Yard).

BUILDINGS AND MAJOR STRUCTURES

There are 195. Of the Academy's major buildings, most of the older ones are of French Renaissance (Beaux Arts) architecture and most of the newer ones are of contemporary architecture.

Alphabetically, they are...

Administration Building: houses various offices, including those of the Superintendent and the Academic Dean and Provost. Completed in 1907.

Alumni Hall (also called the Brigade Activities Center): houses a 6,500-seat multipurpose arena and the Bob Hope Performing Arts Center—with its 2,400-square-foot stage; site of home games for Navy basketball; used for processing new Plebes on I-Day. Completed in 1991.

Bancroft Hall: probably the world's largest dormitory; all midshipmen live there—in its 1,873 residential rooms; has about 4.8 miles of corridors and 33 acres of floor space; also houses many support facilities for midshipmen. In Bancroft as well are the Rotunda (with murals depicting naval engagements) and the Main Office (principal point of contact with midshipmen). King Hall, Memorial Hall, and Smoke Hall are separate parts of Bancroft. Completed in 1906 (the Rotunda and what are now the third and fourth wings) and added to periodically since (fifth and sixth wings in 1920, first and second wings in 1941, seventh and eighth wings in 1960); named for Secretary of the Navy George Bancroft, the individual most responsible for creation of the Naval Academy; now undergoing renovation wing by wing.

Buchanan House: the Superintendent's residence. Completed in 1906; named for Commander Franklin Buchanan, the first Superintendent (and later the commander of the CSS *Virginia,* or *Merrimac,* when it fought the *Monitor*).

Chapel (The Naval Academy Chapel, also the Cathedral of the Navy): has six chaplains; seats 2,500; has five stained-glass windows (Christ Walking on the Water, the Invisible Commission, Sir Galahad, and windows honoring Admirals Sampson and Farragut); has smaller St. Andrew's Chapel downstairs; houses the crypt of John Paul Jones (father of the Navy); the dome is 192 feet high. Completed in 1908, with an addition completed in 1940; renovated and air-conditioned in 1992.

Chauvenet Hall: with its sister building, Michelson Hall, houses the Division of Mathematics and Science. Completed in 1968; named for William Chauvenet, one of the Academy's founding faculty members.

Robert Crown Sailing Center: oversees all Academy sailing activities; on Santee Basin; houses the Intercollegiate Sailing Hall of Fame. Completed in 1974; named for a former Navy League president, Captain Robert Crown.

Dahlgren Hall: similar to the student union at civilian schools; site of dances and other events; houses a hockey rink and a cafeteria and reception area for midshipmen and visitors (the

"Drydock"). Completed in 1903 with its sister building, Mac-donough Hall; named for Rear Admiral John Dahlgren, a Civil War inventor of large-caliber guns.

Halligan Hall: houses the Academy's Public Works, Human Resources, and Supply Departments—as well as the comptroller. Completed in 1903; named for Rear Admiral John Halligan, the first director of the Naval Postgraduate School when it was established at the Academy (1913) in this building.

Halsey Field House: used for sports and physical training; 80,000 square feet; has tennis courts, squash courts, 6,000-seat basketball court, boxing center, 200-meter synthetic track, and body-building equipment. Completed in 1957; named for World War II Fleet Admiral William F. Halsey, Jr.

Hendrix Oceanography Laboratory: located between Severn River and Santee Basin; houses a wet laboratory, circulating tanks, and classrooms. Completed in 1985; named for Captain Charles Hendrix, a submarine and undersea-warfare specialist.

Hubbard Hall: serves as the Academy's boathouse for crew; also used upstairs for social functions; houses the "N" Club for varsity lettermen; on Dorsey Creek. Completed in 1930; the first Academy building named for a living individual: Rear Admiral John Hubbard, stroke for the 1870 crew (Navy's first).

King Hall: part of Bancroft; midshipmen's dining area (or wardroom); 55,000 square feet; 372 tables; can feed entire Brigade in several minutes; serves 12,000 hot meals per day. Named for World War II Fleet Admiral and Chief of Naval Operations Ernest J. King.

Leahy Hall: houses the registrar as well as the admissions and candidate-guidance offices. Completed in 1939; named for Fleet Admiral William Leahy, Chief of Staff to President Roosevelt during World War II.

Lejeune Hall: houses the Academy's primary Olympic-size swimming pool (25 meters by 50 meters, 1.25 million gallons of water) and diving platforms, plus the wrestling center, a weight room, saunas, and the Academy's Athletic Hall of Fame. Completed in 1981, it is the only Academy building named for a Marine—World War I Major General John Lejeune (1888), commandant of the Marine Corps 1920–1929.

Luce Hall: houses the Division of Professional Development and the planetarium. Completed in 1920; named for Naval War College founder (and navigation book author) Admiral Stephen B. Luce.

Macdonough Hall: houses facilities for boxing, fencing, gymnastics, lacrosse, 150-pound football, soccer, swimming, volleyball, and water polo. Completed in 1903 with its sister building, Dahlgren Hall; named for Commodore Thomas Macdonough, who destroyed a British force of 14 ships on Lake Champlain in the War of 1812.

Mahan Hall: until 1973 was the Academy library; now is primarily an area for cultural events (theater and concert). Completed in 1907; named for Rear Admiral Alfred Thayer Mahan, a famed naval biographer, historian, and military theorist whose writings revolutionized strategy and seapower.

Maury Hall: houses Electrical Engineering, Weapons, and Systems Engineering Departments. Completed in 1907; named for pioneer nineteenth-century oceanographer Matthew Fontaine Maury.

Memorial Hall: part of Bancroft; one of the Academy's most hallowed places (midshipmen accord it the reverence and solemnity of a church); dedicated to Navy and Marine heroes and to Academy alumni killed in action or who otherwise have distinguished themselves; contains exhibits and memorabilia; has two massive chandeliers inspired by Versailles; topped by a skylight with 489 panes of glass.

Michelson Hall: with its sister building, Chauvenet Hall, houses the Division of Mathematics and Science. Completed in 1968; named for Academy teacher Albert Michelson, the first American to win the Nobel Prize (1907, in physics—for, among other things, more accurately measuring the speed of light).

Mitscher Hall: houses a chapel, the Chaplain's Center, and an auditorium; located between Bancroft's seventh and eighth wings. Completed in 1960; named for World War II Admiral Marc Mitscher.

Navy–Marine Corps Memorial Stadium: home of Navy football; site for certain other spectator sports and for graduation; has about 30,000 seats; includes one hundred–player locker-room complex named for Rear Admiral Thomas Hamilton, 1927, a former player, coach, and athletic director; located less than a mile from The Yard on Rowe Boulevard, between Taylor and Farragut Avenues; the Brigade marches over for home football games. Completed in 1959.

Nimitz Library: houses 600,000 books, including rare and special collections; also houses the Departments of Economics, Political Science, and Language Studies, plus the archives and a photo lab; can accommodate 1,500 midshipmen reading and studying at the same time. Completed in 1973; named for World War II Pacific Fleet Admiral Chester Nimitz.

Observatory: completed in 1991; contains the telescope, ground by Alvan Clark, from the Academy's old observatory, which was demolished in the early 1900s.

Officers' and Faculty Club: completed in 1905.

Preble Hall: houses the Naval Academy Museum (50,000 items, including most of the Academy's major collections) and the Naval Institute (publisher of books and periodicals related to the Navy, the Marines, the Coast Guard, and the Naval Academy). Completed in 1939; named for the commander of the 1804 attack on the Barbary pirates at Tripoli, Commodore Edward Preble.

Ricketts Hall: houses the athletic-event ticket offices and the offices of football coaches and the Naval Academy Athletic Association (NAAA), plus dormitory rooms for enlisted personnel and visiting teams. Completed in 1966; named for Admiral Claude Ricketts.

Rickover Hall: houses the Division of Engineering and Weapons; contains a large ship-model tow tank and the Academy's largest and most sophisticated laboratories. Completed in 1975; named for Admiral Hyman Rickover, prime mover behind the nuclear-power Navy.

Sampson Hall: houses the Division of Humanities and Social Sciences plus the Departments of English and History, as well as the Academy's writing center. Completed in 1907; named for Spanish-

American War Admiral (and former Superintendent) William T. Sampson.

Satellite Earth Station: installed on Hospital Point in 1988.

Smoke Hall: part of Bancroft. Completed in 1908; takes its name from the function it long served, as a place for midshipmen to gather, talk, and smoke.

Tecumseh Court (T-Court): the area between the Tecumseh monument and the front of Bancroft; used for all formations, including noon meal formations (12:05 Monday through Friday when the temperature is at least 55 degrees); also used for various outdoor gatherings such as major ceremonies and pep rallies.

Visitor Center: officially, the Armel-Leftwich Visitor Center, a $7-million, two-story, public-private facility adjacent to Halsey Field House. Completed in 1995; named for two members of the class of 1953.

Ward Hall: houses the Academy's computer center. Completed in the 1940s; named for Commander James Ward, the first Commandant.

ROADS, WALKWAYS, FIELDS, ETC.

Most of the roads on The Yard (which has 13 miles of them) bear the names of past Superintendents; the major exception is Decatur Road—named for Stephen Decatur, a hero of the War of 1812.

Hill Bridge, over Dorsey Creek, is named for Admiral Harry Hill, a Superintendent.

Porter Road is known as "Captains' Row," for the Academy's highest-ranking officers and their families housed on it. Rodgers and Upshur Roads are known as "Commanders' Rows," for all the commanders and captains and their families housed on them; Upshur, Porter, and Rodgers were early Superintendents. Various lower-ranking officers live in the houses and apartments both to the right of Gate 8 on The Yard (as one leaves The Yard) and across Maryland Route 450 from Gate 8 in Perry Circle; they are primarily Company officers and members of the Academy's faculty and administration.

The Yard has 15 miles of walkways. Two of the major ones, Stribling and Goldsborough, are likewise named for Superintendents.

Fitch Bridge, the footbridge across Dorsey Creek, is named for John Fitch—inventor of the first steam-powered boat (1786).

The Academy has seven named fields. Worden Field, the Academy's parade ground, is named for a Superintendent who also commanded the *Monitor* during the Civil War. Dewey and Farragut Fields are named for famous admirals; Ingram Field and Forrest Sherman Field (also called Hospital Point) are named for a World War II commander of the South Atlantic Fleet and for a Chief of Naval Operations, respectively (both Academy graduates); Lawrence Field (baseball) is named for the captain who said, "Don't give up the ship!"; the adjacent Max F. Bishop Stadium is named for the Academy's 1938–1962 baseball coach; Richmond Kelly Turner Field (covered with synthetic turf, and where PEP is held during Plebe Summer and the 150-pound football team plays its home games), is named for a World War II admiral who commanded the Pacific amphibious force.

Radford Terrace, between Chauvenet and Michelson Halls, is named for Admiral Arthur Radford, chairman of the Joint Chiefs of Staff during the Eisenhower administration.

Santee Basin and Santee Road are named for a wooden frigate assigned to the Academy in 1862—moored in the Severn River for 50 years and used for training and discipline (miscreant midshipmen were quartered—or "brigged"—aboard her, a practice lasting well into the twentieth century).

MONUMENTS

Of the Academy's 75 monuments, the major ones are these:

Mexican: located at roughly the intersection of Stribling and Chapel Walks; erected in 1848.

Herndon: a 21-foot granite obelisk located near the front of the Chapel; erected in 1859.

Tecumseh: located opposite the main entrance to Bancroft Hall; figurehead of the USS *Deleware;* placed at its present site in 1917, and replaced by the current bronze copy in 1930.

Japanese Bell: located on the front left of Tecumseh Court as one faces Bancroft's main entrance; the original installed on The Yard in 1858.

Hirosi Saito: located in front of Luce Hall; installed post-1938.

USS Maine *foremast:* located near Triton Light [see below]; from the ship whose sinking in Havana Harbor began the Spanish-American War (the *Maine's* mainmast is in Arlington National Cemetery—making the *Maine,* some say, the world's longest ship).

Enterprise *Bell:* located on the right of Tecumseh Court as one faces Bancroft's main entrance; from a World War II aircraft carrier; installed in 1951.

Tripolitan: located between Leahy and Preble Halls; the country's first monument to the Navy, it was moved from the U.S. Capitol to its present site in 1860.

Triton Light: located at the corner of the Severn River and Chesapeake Bay seawalls; contains water from the 22 seas the USS *Triton* traversed on its underwater circumnavigation of the globe (its light blinks "4"..."5" honoring the Academy class that donated it).

Macedonian: located at the north end of Stribling Walk; erected in 1924.

Aircraft at the Academy include an N3N seaplane trainer (hanging from Dahlgren's ceiling), an A-4 Skyhawk (opposite Hubbard Hall), and an F-4 Phantom (opposite the entrance to Ricketts Hall).

A 21-foot-long Mark XIV torpedo is located near Triton Light; placed there in 1975, the torpedo memorializes the 52 Academy submariners who died at sea during World War II. An X-1 submarine is located near Ricketts Hall; first used in the mid-1950s experimentally, it exploded in 1958 and was returned to the fleet in 1960 for oceanic research.

HISTORY

The following draws from many sources, two Naval Institute Press books notable among them: Annapolis Today *by Kendall Banning, revised by A. Stuart Pitt [1963], and* The U.S. Naval Academy *by Academy history professor Jack Sweetman [1979].*

1649—Ten Puritan families from Virginia establish a town they call Providence at the mouth of the Severn River.

1670—Providence, since called Town of Procter's and Town of Severn, becomes Anne Arundel Town.

1694—Anne Arundel Town becomes Annapolis—after James II's second daughter, Princess Anne (later Queen); Annapolis becomes capital of the Maryland colony.

1708—Annapolis becomes an incorporated city.

1794—By a two-vote margin, Congress creates a Navy consisting of six frigates (March 27); it also authorizes the President to appoint 48 midshipmen.

1800—President John Adams suggests creation of a naval school.

1808—The War Department purchases 9.75 acres on Windmill Point, the eastern tip of Annapolis—where a stone windmill has stood since 1760; the windmill is replaced by a circular rampart, which is named Fort Severn.

1817—The first training cruise for midshipmen occurs aboard the brig *Prometheus.*

1821—An informal shipboard school for midshipmen, taught by seagoing schoolmasters, is established aboard the frigate *Guerrière* in New York.

1822—A second shipboard naval school is established aboard the frigate *Java* in Norfolk.

1827—The government grade of "passed midshipman," a term for those who have passed their examination for promotion to lieutenant but are awaiting a vacancy to fill, becomes "acting midshipman on probation"—or "acting midshipman."

1833—A third naval school is established at the Boston Navy Yard.

1839—A fourth naval school is established at the Philadelphia Naval Asylum (a home for aging sailors); the Asylum offers a one-year course leading to commissioning in the Navy as a lieutenant; three years later (April 1842) the Asylum will be headed by the distinguished mathematician William Chauvenet, who becomes a leading proponent of a national naval school.

1842—Commander Alexander Mackenzie of the brig *Somers* orders the hanging from the yardarm of acting midshipman Philip Spencer, son of Secretary of War John Spencer, for conspiring to mutiny on board the *Somers* (December 1); the incident heightens public awareness of the need for improvement in the selection, education, and training of would-be naval officers.

1845—Historian George Bancroft becomes Secretary of the Navy (March 11); taking to heart Chauvenet's arguments for a national naval school, Bancroft carries the concept to fruition at last; Captain Isaac Mayo urges locating such a school at the nearly abandoned nine-building Fort Severn, located on Windmill Point at the confluence of the Severn River and Spa Creek in the Annapolis harbor; the Naval School is created; the War Department transfers Fort Severn to the Navy Department (August); the Philadelphia Naval School moves to Annapolis; Secretary Bancroft names Commander Franklin Buchanan the new school's first Superintendent and asks him to draw up a plan of operation (August); Buchanan formally opens the school with an October 10 speech to about 50 midshipmen and a seven-man faculty (four officers and three civilians— including Chauvenet); Buchanan sets a five-year academic/professional program (the first and last years at the school, and the middle three at sea), and fixes minimum and maximum ages for entry at 13 and 16; prospective entrants sit for an exam (October); the school becomes the nation's sole source of naval officers until 1917.

1846—Eighty midshipmen are enrolled at the school—many from the former Philadelphia Asylum School; the new school holds its first ball (January 15); Richmond Aulik, ranked first in his class, becomes the new Naval School's first graduate.

1847—The Academy doubles its land area by the acquisition of adjacent property.

1849—Formation of the first extracurricular organization, the Masqueraders—believed to be the oldest collegiate theater group in the country.

1850—The Naval School officially becomes The United States Naval Academy (July 1) and is placed under the chief of the Bureau of Ordnance and Hydrography; the Academy gets its own uniform, a four-year academic program (interrupted by three years at sea between the end of the second and the beginning of the third years), a 0.0–4.0 marking system (with 2.5 required to pass), a board of visitors, an improved discipline system (with demerits no longer driving down grades), and a Commandant (Lieutenant James Ward, heretofore a faculty member and the Naval School's first executive officer); those enrolled in the first year graduate.

1851—Academy midshipmen take their first summer training cruise, aboard the sloop *Preble,* which is thereafter assigned to the Academy for training purposes; the Secretary of the Navy approves an uninterrupted four-year course of study and training, plus summer cruises; Congress puts itself in the business of appointing midshipmen—heretofore the responsibility of the President and the Secretary of the Navy; the Academy begins calling fourth classmen Plebes, third classmen Youngsters, and second classmen Oldsters.

1852—Formation of the Naval Academy Band, with 13 musicians.

1853—Again the Academy nearly doubles its land area—via (a) acquisition and (b) landfill along both the Severn and Spa Creek.

1854—The Academy holds its first graduation exercise (June 10).

1858—The Lawrence Literary Society becomes the first officially approved midshipman organization.

1861—Because of Civil War hostilities, the Academy moves to Fort Adams, near Newport, Rhode Island (May 13); midshipmen and faculty make the trip aboard the USS *Baltic;* the Annapolis campus is transferred to the War Department for use as a federal campground and military hospital.

1862—"Acting midshipmen" officially become "midshipmen" (July 16).

1865—The Academy returns to Annapolis (September 9); a permanent Academy Marine detachment is formed; the first Farewell Ball is held.

1866—The Academy acquires the Maryland Governor's Mansion and its four accompanying acres.

1867—The Academy buys 10 acres from St. John's College (November 5); the first midshipman publication, *Shakings,* appears—a collection of humorous sketches of Academy life by Midshipman Park Benjamin; the class of 1867 becomes the first to be designated by its year of graduation (heretofore midshipmen have been designated by their year of entrance), and becomes the first to adopt a class badge and class colors; the Academy comes under the authority of the Navy Department (March).

1868—The Academy expands by 67 acres, with the purchase of Strawberry Hill (November).

1869—The first class rings appear.

1870—Congress regrades midshipmen "cadet midshipmen" (July 15); a four-man Navy crew rows its first race against outside competition—the Quaker City Club of Philadelphia.

1872—James Conyers becomes the first black to enter the Academy (September); he stays a year.

1873—The Academy acquires a four-acre tract between College Avenue and Wagner Street; founding of the U.S. Naval Institute (October 9).

1877—Annual midshipman pay is set at $950.

1878—The Paris Exposition issues a certificate to the Academy for providing "the best system of education in the United States."

1882—Congress stipulates that Academy graduates may take commissions in the Marine Corps; Congress reclassifies "cadet midshipmen" as "naval cadets"; the football team plays its first game—against the Clifton Football Club—and wins 8-0 (November 30).

1886—Founding of The Naval Academy Graduates' Association.

1889—The Academy expands with the purchase of 15 acres along College Creek; Congress raises the minimum and maximum ages for incoming midshipmen to 18 and 20, respectively.

1890—Navy wins (24-0) the first Army-Navy football game (at

West Point, November 29); the "N" athletic letter is awarded for the first time; Worden Field opens.

1891—Founding of The Naval Academy Athletic Association by Robert Means Thompson.

1892—The Academy's colors formally are changed from red and white to blue and gold.

1893—A goat named El Cid appears at an Army-Navy football game, won by Navy 6-4, and subsequently a goat is adopted as the Academy mascot—though a dog, two cats, and a carrier pigeon serve brief reigns before Bill the goat's official designation in 1904.

1894—The first edition of the *Lucky Bag* appears (it becomes the Academy's yearbook).

1898—The Navy Department adopts for the Naval Academy the seal (bearing the words "Ex Scientia Tridens") designed by 1867 class member Park Benjamin (January 25).

1899—Based on an ambitious 1896 reconstruction plan by New York architect Ernest Flagg, work begins on new Academy buildings (March 28).

1901—Work begins on Bancroft Hall.

1902—The Academy expands via the purchase of 12 acres; Congress abolishes the designation "naval cadet" and restores the designation "midshipman" (July 1).

1903—Dahlgren and Macdonough Halls open (March 7); Halligan Hall is completed.

1904—Admiral Dewey lays the cornerstone for the Chapel; Bill the goat becomes the Academy mascot.

1905—Completion of the Officers' Club; *Reef Points* first appears (October 24).

1906—Bancroft and Buchanan House are completed; sleeve insignia are adopted to distinguish the four classes; (a) the forward pass is used for the first time in an Army-Navy game and (b) "Anchors Aweigh" is sung for the first time at an Army-Navy game.

1907—The Administration Building and the Naval Academy Hospital open; Mahan, Sampson, and Maury Halls are completed

(Mahan serves as the library until 1973); an Academy crew appears in its first intercollegiate regatta (Poughkeepsie, New York); varsity basketball is established.

1908—The Chapel, with a capacity of 1,600, is dedicated (May).

1909—Old Fort Severn is demolished; varsity tennis is established.

1910—The Academy buys its own 180-acre dairy across the Severn at Greenbury Point; varsity wrestling is established.

1911—Varsity swimming is established.

1912—Congress drops the requirement of a two-year sea-duty probation for Academy graduates before receiving their commissions—stipulating that commissions shall be offered at graduation (May 12); graduating midshipmen toss their hats into the air at their commissioning ceremony, establishing a tradition that endures.

1913—With construction of a concrete bridge across College (later Dorsey) Creek, the Academy completes its 1899 rebuilding plan; a crypt beneath the Chapel becomes the new resting place of the body of John Paul Jones (January 26); the first issue of *The Log* appears (October 31) as a weekly newspaper (contrary to its later incarnation as a monthly humor magazine); the Academy moves its dairy to a 771-acre tract at Gambrills.

1915—The practice of allowing Academy graduates to accept Marine Corps commissions, suspended since 1897, is resumed; formation of the Hellcats, which becomes (in 1925) the Drum and Bugle Corps.

1916—Congress approves the present system of appointing midshipmen.

1917—The total number of incumbent midshipmen each Senator and Congressman may have at the Academy at any time is raised to five (where it remains); the wooden figurehead of Delaware Indian Chief Tamanend, salvaged in 1866 from the scuttled 74-gun *Delaware* (burned in Norfolk in 1861 to prevent its capture by the Confederates), is placed (September 5) near Bancroft Hall (the midshipmen later dub the figurehead "Tecumseh"—a famous Shawnee chief).

1920—Luce Hall is built.

1922—The Bandstand near the Chapel is built.

1923—Establishment of the Department of Physical Training; Lawrence Field is dedicated (for baseball).

1925—The Academy adopts "Navy Blue and Gold" as its hymn; the Drum and Bugle Corps is formed from the Hellcats, a group established in 1915.

1929—Work begins on Hubbard Hall (the boathouse) on the north bank of College (formerly Graveyard, later Dorsey) Creek; the Chapel gets a copper roof.

1930—The Association of American Universities accredits the Academy (October 25); a bronze copy replaces the original wooden figurehead of Tamanend ("Tecumseh") at its present location in front of Bancroft.

1931—The Academy begins issuing Bachelor of Science degrees.

1933—Congress authorizes the Superintendent (May 25) to confer the Bachelor of Science degree on all midshipmen who have graduated since formal accreditation of the Academy in 1930.

1939—Congress authorizes the Superintendent to confer the Bachelor of Science degree on all the Academy's living graduates; Preble Hall opens.

1940—The Chapel nave is extended to accommodate 2,500 worshipers (dedicated in June).

1941—The Academy grows by 29.5 acres (to 245 acres) by the dredging of silt from the Severn River.

1941—Construction begins on Ward Hall.

1947—For the first time, first class midshipmen are permitted to own cars and—if seven miles from the Academy—to drink alcohol; the Middle Atlantic States Association of Colleges and Secondary Schools accredits the Naval Academy.

1949—Midshipman Wesley Brown becomes the Academy's first black graduate.

1950—The Academy holds its first open house for parents of Plebes.

1951—The honor concept goes into effect; the Naval Post-graduate School, established at the Academy in 1913, moves to Monterey, California (November 21).

1952—The mess hall, known today as King Hall, gets a new wing.

1957—Halsey Field House is dedicated (June 5).

1958—For the class of 1962, the Academy converts to using Scholastic Aptitude Test (SAT) scores in the admissions process instead of administering its own exam.

1959—The Academy institutes a new academic program that includes advanced placement plus electives that may be taken in addition to the fixed curriculum; 28,135-seat Navy–Marine Corps Memorial Stadium is dedicated (September 26).

1960—The Academy expands by 54.5 acres by the dredging of silt from the Severn River and Spa Creek, thereby creating Dewey and Farragut Fields; Bancroft's seventh and eighth wings are completed.

1962—In the first officially recorded timing of the event, Midshipman Edwin Linz (1965) scales Herndon Monument in (apparently) a record 3:00 minutes (June 6).

1963—The Academy approves (a) creation of the post of Academic Dean, and (b) initiation of the Trident Scholar program (for the class of 1964).

1964—The Academy adds a minors program, thereby abandoning a fixed curriculum for all midshipmen; it also inaugurates letter-grade equivalents in conjunction with the numerical grading system established in 1850.

1965—The number of Companies increases from 24 to 36; the Academy creates the position of Dean of Admissions.

1966—Ricketts Hall is completed.

1968—Chauvenet and Michelson Halls are completed.

1969—The class of 1972 scales Herndon monument in a new record time of 1 minute 30 seconds (May); the Academy inaugurates the majors program, offering 24 majors (September).

1972—Lieutenant Commander Georgia Clark becomes the first female member of the faculty; First Classmen are required to pass the Professional Competency Review exam as a condition of graduation (December); an extra semester (the four-and-a-half-year stretch program) is approved for those in academic difficulty; the Chief of Naval Operations and the Commandant of the Marine Corps agree that the Marines will be entitled to offer commissions to up to one-sixth of each graduating class, and in return will fill one-sixth of the Academy's faculty and staff positions; in addition, a Marine colonel—serving as senior Marine officer—will head up an academic division.

1973—Nimitz Library opens (September).

1974—The Robert Crown Sailing Center opens (spring).

1975—Rickover Hall opens; a student union opens in Dahlgren Hall.

1976—The first women (81) are inducted (July 9)—into the class of 1980; Midshipman Mason Reddix becomes the first black Brigade Commander.

1977—Lieutenant Susan Stephens becomes the first female Company Officer.

1980—The first women graduate.

1981—The Bancroft wardroom is officially dedicated to the memory of Fleet Admiral Ernest King, Chief of Naval Operations and commander-in-chief of the U.S. fleet during World War II; the Interfaith Chapel in Mitscher is dedicated (August).

1982—The Lejeune Physical Education Center opens (April).

1984—Construction of a replacement bridge over Dorsey Creek is completed; construction begins on the 2,400-niche Columbarium for crematory interment; Kristine Holereid becomes the first woman at any service academy to graduate first in her class.

1987—The Academy authorizes a minor in foreign languages (December); Commander Marsha Evans becomes the first female Battalion Officer; construction begins on the 150,000-square-foot Alumni Hall; creation of the Objectives Review Board (ORB), consisting of about 20 senior Academy officers (and the Brigade Commander) to advise the Superintendent on matters of organization, curriculum, and professional training.

1988—Installation of a 12-meter X-Y drive parabolic dish is completed on Hospital Point for the tracking of orbital satellites.

1989—The Academy installs its fifth Academic Dean (Robert Shapiro), who later becomes its first Provost as well.

1991—Alumni Hall (costing $17 million in private funds and $13 million in public funds), along with the Bob Hope Performing Arts Center, is dedicated and first used for the processing of new Plebes on I-Day; dedication of the Observatory containing an Alvan Clark telescope (June); Midshipman Juliane Gallina becomes the first female Brigade Commander.

1992—Heating, ventilating, and air-conditioning of the Chapel is completed (November); at Navy–Marine Corps Stadium a 100-player locker facility named for former player, coach, and athletic director Thomas Hamilton, 1927, is dedicated; Hubbard Hall is renovated; an electrical engineering exam is compromised (December 14), resulting during the subsequent 18 months in (a) the punishment and retention of 47 midshipmen, and (b) the separation of 24—all in the class of 1994.

1994—The $7-million public-private Armel-Leftwich Visitor Center, named for two members of the class of 1953, is dedicated adjacent to Halsey Field House (May 12).

1995—A $1-million baseball clubhouse with press and locker facilities is dedicated and named for William H. G. FitzGerald, 1931, a former Academy baseball player; pregnancy policies are modified and alcohol policies are toughened; the Academy celebrates the 150th anniversary of its founding.

3 / ACADEMICS

The Naval Academy's academics rank among the nation's toughest. They are driven by a core curriculum consisting of required courses in engineering, the natural sciences, math, and the humanities. Given the strong technical emphasis of the core curriculum in what remains fundamentally an engineering school, all graduating midshipmen—whatever their major—receive a Bachelor of Science degree.

Overall, the curriculum is highly structured. Throughout most of the Academy's history, midshipmen could not choose any courses. In 1959 the Academy inaugurated electives; in 1969 it converted to a system of majors. Although about half the Plebes begin the academic year with some form of advanced placement or Academy validation in one or more courses, Plebes have just about no choice regarding the courses they take. Choice, specifically regarding electives and courses in the major, increases as midshipmen advance toward graduation.

The Academy offers about 300 courses per semester.

MAJORS AND DIVISIONS

Plebes select one of 18 majors toward the end of Plebe Year. Depending on one's chosen major, a midshipman must take anywhere from 27 to 45 credit hours in his or her major. The majors are:

Aerospace Engineering	Marine Engineering
Chemistry	Mathematics
Computer Science	Mechanical Engineering
Economics	Naval Architecture
Electrical Engineering	Ocean Engineering
English	Oceanography
General Engineering	Physics
General Science	Political Science
History	Systems Engineering

The Academy has three academic divisions:

Engineering and Weapons, with five departments offering eight majors:

Aerospace Engineering
Electrical Engineering
General Engineering
Marine Engineering
Mechanical Engineering
Naval Architecture
Ocean Engineering
Systems Engineering

Midshipmen in any of those eight majors—called Division I majors—constitute about 40 percent of the Academy's upperclassmen. Non-majors must take 20–23 hours of core courses in this division (among them: electrical engineering, thermodynamics, strengths of materials, mechanics, and control systems).

Mathematics and Science, with five departments offering six majors:

Chemistry
Computer Science
General Science
Mathematics
Oceanography
Physics

Midshipmen in any of those six majors—called Division II majors—constitute about 24 percent of the Academy's upperclassmen. Courses in this division make up the largest segment of courses in the core curriculum, and the Mathematics Department is the largest of the Academy's academic departments.

Humanities and Social Sciences, with five departments offering four majors:

Economics
English
History
Political Science

Those majoring in Economics, English, History, or Political Science—called Division III or "bull" majors—must take or validate a minimum of four semesters (12 credits) in French, German, Japanese, Russian, or Spanish. Language courses are given by the division's Department of Language Studies, which offers minors in all five languages, but no majors. To earn a minor in a foreign language, a midshipman must have a 3.0 average in his or her language courses and complete 12 credits in advanced-level courses.

Midshipmen in Division III majors represent about 36 percent of the Academy's upperclassmen. At one time the Academy imposed a cap on the number of midshipmen who could enroll in Group III majors, but no longer.

The Academy has a fourth division, the *Division of Professional Development,* which is partly academic and partly professional—that is, it aids in the training of Navy and Marine Corps officers.

Widely known as ProDev, it consists of two teaching departments: (1) Leadership and Law, and (2) Seamanship and Navigation.

Those departments offer core-curriculum and elective courses. In addition, there are three nonacademic departments: Sailing, Technical Programs, and Professional Programs.

Professional Programs instructs midshipmen in things military and nonacademic. In that capacity it oversees such things as (a) Plebe indoctrination (Indoc); (b) professional training and the annual administration of Professional Competency Review (PCR) tests of retained military knowledge; (c) summer training; and (d) career information and Service Assignment. This department also provides instruction in the essentials of sailing. And it operates and maintains classrooms, labs, and equipment for ProDev educational programs—for example: software, trainers, simulators, command information centers, YPs (Yard Patrol craft), and the planetarium.

HONORS AND GRADUATE PROGRAMS

There are 10 honor societies.

Selected majors—notably English, History, Economics, Math, Oceanography, and Political Science—have honors programs. Midshipmen who satisfactorily complete such programs graduate with honors. To qualify for graduation with honors in a major, a midshipman must have (a) a CQPR of 3.0, (b) a CQPR of 3.5 in courses in his or her major, (c) a 2.5 CQPR in professional courses, and (d) no Ds or Fs on the final transcript [see below].

The Trident Scholar program allows some midshipmen with particular academic strengths—and standing in the top 10 percent of their class—to take reduced course loads in their final year to accommodate research and the writing of a thesis under an adviser's guidance. The number of Trident Scholars varies from year to year, ranging generally between 3 and 15.

VGEP (the Voluntary Graduate Education Program) allows up to 20 top academic performers who complete their academic requirements by the end of the first semester of their First Class year to enroll in graduate classes at any of seven nearby universities. Such midshipmen can thus graduate with their class, receive their commissions, and thereafter earn Master's degrees within seven months before going to their first duty assignments.

Midshipmen may also be selected for a variety of graduate programs and scholarships—among them a medical school program for up to 15 graduates, the Burke program, the Cox fund, and Olmsted, FitzGerald, and Pownall scholarships.

About 80 percent of Academy graduates pursue graduate study at some time. Those taking funded graduate programs at either a military or civilian graduate school generally must commit to two additional years of active duty for each year of graduate study.

GRADES, ETC.

A simple subject made almost unintelligibly complex.

Teachers award letter grades, without pluses and minuses—but then numbers take over.

For purposes of calculating 6-week, 12-week, 18-week (semester), or overall averages, every letter grade has a Quality Point Equivalent (QPE):

$$A = 4$$
$$B = 3$$
$$C = 2$$
$$D = 1$$
$$F = 0$$

A midshipman computes his or her Quality Point Ratio (QPR) in the following manner:

(1) For each course, multiply the QPE by its credit value (usually the number of times the course meets per week). (Example: If the midshipman has a C in calculus and calculus meets four times per week, multiply 2—a C equaling 2 points—by 4, for four hours a week.)

(2) Add the resulting products.

(3) Divide that sum by the sum of the credit values.

(4) That number, rounded to two decimal places, is the QPR— generally expressed for 6, 12, and 18 weeks as an SQPR (Semester Quality Point Ratio) or overall as a CQPR (Cumulative Quality Point Ratio). The latter, adjusted each semester to reflect semester grades, is often called—

phonetically—a *Kyoomie* or *Kyooper.* (In cases of repeated courses in which the original course grade was a D or an F, the repeated course grade replaces the earlier grade in the CQPR.) Summer-school grades are incorporated into one's CQPR.

Yet that is not all. Although an academic GPA or CQPR is important, it is only 65 percent of the story. A midshipman's class standing, or Order of Merit, reflects not only academics but his or her grades in conduct, military performance, physical education, and athletics. Only when all those grades are combined with the academic average (which alone does not reflect them) does a midshipman arrive at his or her overall CQPR and Order of Merit—on the basis of which certain privileges are dispensed.

Midshipmen performing especially well may make one or more of three lists. The requirements for each are:

—Superintendent's List (made by about 6 percent of midshipmen): semester QPR of at least 3.4, with no semester grades below a C; an A in military performance; an A in conduct; at least a B in physical education. (Those qualifying may wear a gold star on certain uniforms.)

—Dean's List (made by about 6 percent of midshipmen): Semester QPR of at least 3.4, with no failures in any course or professional area. (Those qualifying may wear a bronze star on the flap of their left breast pocket of certain working uniforms.)

—Commandant's List (made by about 22 percent of midshipmen): semester QPR of at least 2.9; at least a B in military performance; an A in conduct; at least a B in physical education. (Those qualifying wear no special insignia, but may, as upperclassmen, be awarded extra liberty.)

In addition, at graduation those in the top 10 percent of the Order of Merit receive their degrees "with distinction." Those below the top 10 percent yet achieving 75 percent of the maximum aggregate multiple receive their degrees "with merit."

Grades go to parents each semester—provided that their midshipman has authorized the Academy to send them. Without such authorization, the Academy will not mail out grades, and parents may never know how their midshipman is doing.

BRIEF POINTS

Academic Adviser—Each Plebe is assigned an adviser during Plebe Summer. Then, when selecting a major in the spring of Plebe Year, he or she is assigned a new adviser for the next three years from the department of his or her major.

Academic Board—By law, it meets every semester. It consists of the Superintendent, the Commandant, the Dean, the heads of the four divisions, and (as a nonvoting member who serves as secretary) the Dean of Admissions; the Athletic Director is also present to offer advice regarding midshipman athletics. The board considers midshipmen having academic (and other) trouble. Technically, those in such trouble are automatically separated from the Academy. The board recommends various courses of action: probation, summer school, extension of the normal graduation date by a semester, or separation; midshipmen with information not formerly available to the board may appeal its decision to separate, and in those cases the board may interview the appealing midshipmen. Academic discharge is likely if in any semester a midshipman (a) has an average below 1.5, (b) fails two (or more) courses, (c) does not remove an academic probation from the previous semester, (d) falls two or more courses behind where he or she should be in his or her major, or (e) does not complete stipulated academic requirements for graduation.

Academic Deficiency—Midshipmen with academic averages of less than 2.0 (a C) in any six-week grading period are considered in academic difficulty: The term used widely at the Academy is "Unsat" (for Unsatisfactory). Those upperclassmen with averages below 2.15 in any six-week grading period are not permitted to take weekends during the following grading period: They're "Non-Weekend Eligible." What's more, there's academic probation for any midshipman (a) with a CQPR below 2.0 at the end of any semester, or (b) with an SQPR below 2.0 in any two consecutive semesters: such midshipmen are technically separated and are considered by the Academic Board to determine whether retention is warranted. A broad range of other academic failings can land a midshipman in academic or other trouble—facing serious questions about retention.

Accreditation—The Academy is accredited by the Middle States Association of Colleges and Secondary Schools. Where available, its majors are also accredited by discipline groups.

Attrition—For all reasons (that is, not just academic reasons), about 25 percent of those enrolled fail to graduate—giving the Academy about a 75-percent graduation (or retention) rate. Nationally, for all colleges, that four-year graduation rate is well below 50 percent.

Class Day—It contains seven 50-minute periods—four in the morning and three after lunch—Monday through Friday; there are no Saturday classes. For the most part, the seventh period is not used except for three-period labs and class-wide exams; for portions of the spring and fall it is used for marching drills on Mondays and for parades on Wednesdays. At night, Sunday through Friday, the hours from 7:30 P.M. to 11:00 P.M. are reserved for study.

Class Size—Average number in a class: 17.5; the number usually falls somewhere between 10 and 22.

Computers—The Academy issues each Plebe a computer at the end of Plebe Summer. During their years at the Academy, midshipmen purchase their computers through payroll deduction, and keep them upon graduation.

Course Load—Every midshipman must take at least 15 credit hours per semester; some take as many as 21 or 22. During their four years at the Academy, midshipmen take a minimum of about 140 credit hours—considerably more (perhaps 25 to 35 percent more) such hours than students at most civilian colleges. Midshipmen add to this load with professional and leadership courses, military performance, drill, physical education, etc.

Dual Major—It's possible, and may be undertaken with approval of the Dean. And some midshipmen do it. But it's tough.

Exams—The Academy is on the semester system. Exams are held before Christmas vacation (or leave) and in May. Exams generally last three hours. In most cases, midshipmen may depart for Christmas vacation following their last exam; they may also depart for End-of-Semester Leave following their last exam in May, but usually must return to the Academy for general military training (called Intersessional) prior to the beginning of Commissioning Week.

Faculty—The Academy has about 600 full-time faculty members. Of that number, (a) about 15 percent are women, and (b) about 50 percent are civilian. There are no graduate teaching assistants. Seventy percent of the civilian faculty is tenured; the civilian faculty's average number of years of service on the faculty is 12.3 (members of the military faculty, of course, rotate through). About 82 percent of the civilian faculty have Ph.D.s (except in physical education, Ph.D.s have been required of all new civilian faculty members since the 1960s); about 66 percent of the military faculty have advanced degrees. The faculty-student ratio is about 1:7.

Graduation Requirements—A cumulative grade point average of 2.0, a C (beginning with the class of 1967: prior to then the requirement was 2.5); 140 credit hours; complete or validate all the stipulated courses in the selected major; satisfy all academic, military, and physical-education requirements. Contrary to widespread belief, neither Ds—even in one's major—nor final-semester grades averaging below 2.0 automatically prevent a Firstie (senior) from graduating.

Help—Midshipmen have a variety of formal options for academic assistance—among them: (1) voluntary or mandatory Extra Instruction (EI) from any instructor during the class day or at night; and (2) help through the Academic Counseling Center, the Writing Center, math labs, and midshipmen tutors.

Probation—Midshipmen may find themselves on academic probation for a variety of reasons—generally if they have low CQPRs or if they flunk a physical education class. In the words of one official statement on the matter: "The purpose of academic probation is to warn midshipmen their [academic] performance is below the required standards and significant improvement will be required to justify further retention at the Naval Academy." They remove themselves from probation by clearing their academic deficiencies [see above in this listing].

Summer School—A possibility in five cases: (1) for makeup in some failed courses; (2) for raising a D; (3) for enrichment; (4) for acceleration; and (5) for those who want to take courses to lighten their academic load during the coming year. About one-quarter of returning midshipmen take Summer School courses. Midshipmen may not attend Summer School in place of their Summer Training obligations, but only during those portions of summer leave when they do not have Summer Training.

BRIEFER POINTS
For a full definition of the following terms, see the glossary.

Academic Accountability
Academic Log
Academic Tracking Sheets
Advisory Board
Aero
Anchor
Attrition Classes
Axe Board (or Ac Board)
Boats
Bull Major
Cables
Civilian
Core Curriculum
Course Policy Statement
Division I, Division II, Division III
Double-E
GPA
Gravy
Mapper
Matrix
Mech-E
Mo Board
Monterey

Narc
Nav
NPGS
NPS
Ocean-E
Order of Merit
Priority
Registration
    (or Pre-Registration)
SCUM
Section Leader
Ships
Ships and Aircraft
Six-N
Star (verb)
Steam
Teacher Evals
Thermo
Trucker's English
Validate
X-week
Youngster
Zenith

4 / **MILITARY MATTERS**

For those unfamiliar with the Naval Academy, its military aspect ranks high among its many mysteries.

This is the aspect that, more than any other, distinguishes the Academy from civilian colleges; this is the aspect making life there nearly unique. Although today the Academy produces only about 17 percent of all new naval officers (collegiate NROTC programs currently produce about 23 percent, and Officer Candidate School [OCS] about 16 percent), it is fundamentally the Navy's college. So not surprisingly, the military side of the school is dominant—even controlling.

The Academy's near-synonym for *military* is *professional,* but the two words connote slight differences: *military* is the broader word, meaning the non-civilian regimen; *professional* is narrower, suggesting the squaring away of midshipmen in terms of military bearing, performance, attitude, and knowledge of the naval profession. Military/professional training begins—big time—on Induction Day, and lasts for the duration. The Division of Professional Development (ProDev) is one of the Academy's most notable, and influential, aspects: By and large, it oversees the more than 2,000 hours (including approximately 45 semester hours in class) of military/professional training given every midshipman while at the Academy.

Officers and upperclassmen continuously evaluate a midshipman's professional (military) aptitude (or "grease"); they evaluate it—for instance—on inspections, on attitude and bearing and general behavior, and on annual Professional Competency Review tests (PCRs). The resulting performance grades constitute about 25 percent of a midshipman's class rank (or Order of Merit). Those not measuring up may find themselves on the road home.

BANCROFT

The crucible for this training is not the parade field—though drill is a dreary constant. It is Bancroft Hall.

Midshipmen used to call Bancroft "Mother B." Now it's usually just "The Hall." And it is where practically everything happens.

Bancroft is the vast dormitory housing all midshipmen—no exceptions. They dwell in rooms there. They eat in a part of it, King Hall. They are reminded of Navy and Marine traditions by another part of it—the revered Memorial Hall.

They study there, are inspected there, are trained and disciplined there, do pranks there, do chow calls there, and form up there during cold or inclement weather. In its basement they buy books and uniforms, shop at the Naval Academy Store (often called the Mid Store), do their banking and telephoning, make their travel arrangements, get their hair cut and shaped, take their uniforms for tailoring or cleaning and their shoes for re-soling, get their cavities filled and their broken arms set, pick up packages, and mail their letters.

Currently undergoing extensive renovations one wing at a time, Bancroft is probably the world's largest dormitory—with a current value listed at $1.2 billion. It has eight wings, 1,873 rooms, nearly five miles of hallway, five floors (plus two basement levels), and 33 acres of floor space. The budget for operating and maintaining Bancroft runs to $3 million per year.

Because Bancroft is a principal training area for individuals who one day will experience shipboard life, it carries gray-hull nomenclature. Its floors are *decks,* its walls *bulkheads,* its ceilings *overheads;* its stairways are *ladders,* its hallways *passageways,* its drinking fountains *scuttlebutts.* Midshipmen stand watch there. Plebes wishing to enter an upperclassman's room, as well as midshipmen wishing to enter an officer's office, "request permission to come aboard."

Bancroft's 55,000-square-foot dining area—or wardroom—is T-shaped King Hall, which prepares 12,000 hot meals per day. In one hour the kitchen can fry a ton of shrimp or broil 3,000 hamburgers; at one time it can cook 750 gallons of soup or 320 turkeys weighing 12 to 16 pounds each. In a typical day, it might serve 1,000 gallons of milk, a ton of green vegetables, two tons of meat and another two tons of potatoes, 720 pies, 1,200 loaves of bread, and 300 gallons of ice cream. King Hall has 372 tables (which always carry peanut butter and jelly). Most midshipmen eat with their Squad at Squad Tables, although in-season varsity athletes sometimes eat (though no special food) with their teammates at Team Tables. Breakfast and dinner are buffet; lunch is served.

THE CLASSES

The Academy does not use conventional collegiate names. Instead, the names are these:

Freshman:	Fourth Class (usually called a Plebe)
Sophomore:	Third Class (usually called a Youngster)
Junior:	Second Class (usually called—in order of frequency—a Second Class, Second Classman)
Senior:	First Class (usually called—in order of frequency —a Firstie, First Class, First Classman)

Their respective military duties:

Plebes:	make the transition from civilian/high-school life, learn about the Navy and Marines, learn how to perform under pressure
Youngsters:	help the Second Class train the Plebes and supplement their knowledge
Second Class:	train the Plebes
First Class:	(a) oversee Plebe training, (b) run the Companies and report to the Company Officers, and (c) assist in running the Brigade.

PLEBES

As the last in—the newest midshipmen on the block—Plebes stand at the bottom of the heap. Having been for the most part outstanding in high school, they enter the Naval Academy and are immediately reduced to insignificance and near-nothingness; certain "rights" are withdrawn, to be returned later as privileges.

Plebes are permitted almost no property (essentially only toilet articles, a watch, an alarm clock, a calculator, and snapshots). Other possibilities: a small lamp, a small fan, special athletic equipment (such as lacrosse sticks or tennis racquets), a book or two, and limited clothing. Those things not worn must be carried on I-Day and stored thereafter, and may cause more grief than they are worth; they might best be sent later when the new midshipman asks for them.

Plebes are accorded practically no privileges and certainly no prestige. And from the moment they are shorn on I-Day, their egos suffer systematic indignities. They are officially allowed to date on precisely four weekends during the academic year—plus during Commissioning Week. They deal with a lot of don'ts, notably the prohibitions against the possession of cars or anything electronic (or battery-powered) that emits sound.

Plebe Summer, which consists primarily of physical training and military indoctrination, is tough. So is Plebe Year—particularly that portion called the Dark Ages, following Christmas vacation. Candidates (or appointees) become Plebes and members of the Fourth Class on Induction Day. At the Herndon ceremony in May they finally shed the stigma *Plebe* and remain members of the Fourth Class only—until graduation several days later, when they become members of the Third Class, or Youngsters. There is debate about that, however: Some say Fourth Classmen do not become Youngsters until they see the Chapel dome upon returning from their Youngster cruise.

BRIGADE ORGANIZATION

All midshipmen constitute the Brigade of Midshipmen.

The Brigade is divided into a number of constituent parts—principally:

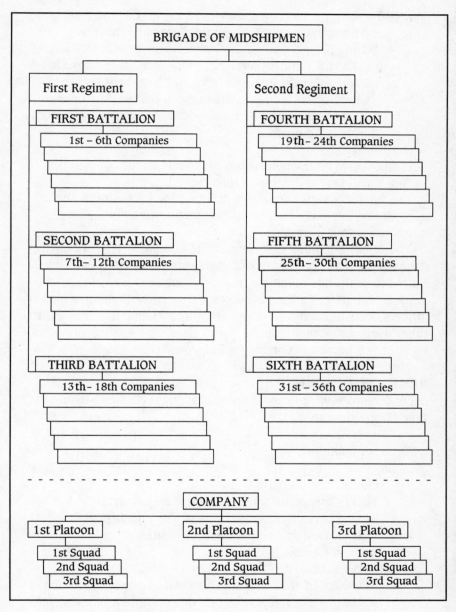

How the Brigade is organized (from a schematic in CSORM).

—Two Regiments (Companies 1–18 are in the First Regiment, and Companies 19–36 are in the Second Regiment).
(During Plebe Summer, the Plebes are organized into what is called the Fourth Class Regiment—consisting of two battalions, called the Port and Starboard Battalions.)
—Six Battalions (the First Battalion comprises Companies 1–6, the Second Battalion comprises companies 7–12, etc.).
—Thirty-six Companies.

Further, each Company consists of three Platoons.
And each Platoon consists of three Squads.
The numbers vary because of attrition, but each Squad, the elemental unit, generally has 12 midshipmen—one or two First Class, and three or four from each of the others.
The major administrative unit is the Company. Each Company generally has about 120 midshipmen—about 30 from each class. Each Company has a commissioned Company Officer and a Company Commander (a Firstie). Except for out-of-Company megastripers, midshipmen may room only in a "Company area" with other members of their Company and class. The method of scrambling Plebes into other Companies frequently changes.

RANK AND INSIGNIA

All midshipmen wear insignia designating their class or—within the First Class—their rank.

Class insignia:
  Sleeves:
      Plebes: no insignia
      Youngsters: one slanted gold stripe on left sleeve
      Second Class: two slanted gold stripes on left sleeve
      First Class: a star and at least one horizontal gold stripe on both sleeves
  Shoulder Boards:
      Members of the Second, Third, and Fourth classes have gold stripes corresponding to those on their sleeves, plus an anchor; members of the First Class have a star and stripes corresponding to those on their sleeves.

Collars:
    Plebes: no devices
    Youngsters: anchor on right collar only
    Second Class: anchor on left and right collar
    First Class: one to six gold stripes on both collars
Upperclassmen also wear shoulder insignia on their raincoats:
    Plebes: nothing
    Youngsters: an anchor pin on the right shoulder
    Second Class: anchor pins on both shoulders
    First Class: eagle pins on both shoulders

All classes wear ribbons, medals, or warfare specialty pins (the last either from prior enlistment or from summer training) over their left breast pocket. Those entitled to a Superintendent's List gold star, a Dean's List bronze star, or a varsity N wear them on the flap of the left breast pocket (Superintendent's stars are also worn above the anchors that midshipmen wear on their SDB lapels or on the collars of their FDBs or Service Dress Whites). Those in the Color Company or in the Drum and Bugle Corps wear, respectively, an E or a bugle on their uniforms.

MIRs, or midshipmen in ranks, wear a horizontal stripe with an anchor on each shoulder board; these are Firsties graduating later than their class.

STRIPERS

Within the Brigade, primarily within the First Class, certain midshipmen (about one-tenth of the Firsties) hold one-semester officer rank corresponding to their duties in the Brigade or in their Regiment, Battalion, Company, Platoon, or Squad.

All Firsties wear one star and one horizontal stripe on their sleeves and shoulder boards; they are called midshipman ensigns. These are the designated ranks for stripers; all wear one star plus...

Two stripes:	midshipman lieutenant junior grade
Three stripes:	midshipman lieutenant
Four stripes:	midshipman lieutenant commander
Five stripes:	midshipman commander
Six stripes:	midshipman captain

The Brigade Commander, who wears six stripes, is the top-ranking midshipman. He or she is assisted by his or her regimental commanders and other stripers. Stripers are selected through a complex process based on interviews, evaluations, and their Academy records. Striper billets, or positions, are for one semester only. In nearly all cases, no Firsties except Brigade Commanders will wear a total of more than six stripes during the year.

In addition, as an extension of the chain of command, there are non-Firstie stripers—Second Classmen who assist First Classmen with the administration of their Companies and the Brigade. They wear no special insignia.

UNIFORMS

Uniforms occupy a major place in a midshipman's life, and beyond. Some general comments:

Midshipmen generally rotate into and out of seasonal uniforms when the rest of the Navy does; for the most part, their uniforms correspond to those worn Navy-wide: white in warm and hot weather, Navy blue (or black) in cool and cold.

During Plebe Summer, Plebes wear white works—the closest thing the Academy has to a white Cracker Jack sailor suit. At the Academy in the summer, upperclass midshipmen wear either summer whites or short-sleeved summer khakis.

During the academic year, midshipmen on The Yard wear their working uniforms—summer working blues (short-sleeved) or winter working blues (long-sleeved).

At night or outside The Yard, they must wear summer whites or service dress blues (SDBs). For more formal occasions, they wear either (a) full dress whites (choker whites) during the day, (b) dinner dress whites and dinner dress blues at night, or (c) for the most formal occasions, full dress whites or full dress blues (chokers, or FDBs).

Those are the major uniforms, though there are a number of others. In addition, midshipmen have a seemingly limitless collection of uniform clothing and paraphernalia: infantry dress, dungarees, and PE gear; a three-button reefer (similar to a Navy pea-coat) and a four-button overcoat; corfams, sneakers, raincoats, garrison caps, and fleet SWO sweaters worn with soft shoulder boards and velcro nametags.

All midshipmen must wear their uniforms at all times except (a) when at their sponsor's house or with their parents in private or (b) when on an authorized weekend or leave. Firsties and Second Class on such a weekend or leave may wear civilian clothes when entering or leaving The Yard.

Midshipmen may wear only their N sweater with civilian clothes; in place of a coat (and without a cover) they may also wear N sweaters with summer working blue uniforms, winter working blues, and service dress blues.

DISCIPLINE

The Academy is a stressful, taxing environment in which inappropriate behavior can and does occur.

Honor offenses—primarily lying, cheating, and stealing—likely will result in dismissal, called separation. Conduct offenses result in disciplinary measures (restriction, extra duty, or tours), but serious ones may result in separation as well. The difference: By and large, conduct offenses are deemed correctable by punishment, while honor offenses are not.

All midshipmen are given conduct and performance grades (A–F), with F indicating the near-certainty of separation; conduct and performance grades are reflected in Order of Merit. Conduct grades are based on the number of demerits a midshipman has received. Performance grades are given according to how midshipmen are ranked by their superiors within their Company (top, middle, or bottom third); performance grades, which are both objective and subjective, incorporate everything from drill and leadership and room appearance to athletics and extracurriculars and military bearing.

A midshipman accused of a conduct infraction is "fried." To be fried means—in civilian terms—to be charged, indicted, put on report. Upon investigation, the fry may be dropped by one of the commissioned officers, or its disposition may be some form of punishment; sometimes fries are resolved by midshipmen on the Company staff.

In cases of alleged honor offenses, the Brigade Honor Committee comes into play. It consists of midshipmen-elected honor stripers who serve year-round; some are elected at the Brigade level, some at the Battalion level, and some at the Company level. The committee's chairman reviews each case and determines whether to counsel the individual or to refer the case to an honor board consisting of members of the committee. If an honor board finds the allegations in a given case likely to be true, the honor committee refers the case to the Commandant. If the case results in a recommendation from the Commandant for separation, it then goes to the Superintendent and then—for final disposition—to the Secretary of the Navy.

Alleged conduct offenses are dealt with administratively, in a nonjudicial fashion, as they are in the fleet. There are separation-level conduct offenses, but most midshipmen who commit them are disciplined and retained as members of the Brigade. In some cases involving separable offenses, the Academy sanctions probation as an alternative.

Midshipmen serve their punishments by serving either "tours" or "restriction."

Tours (actually, "area tours") are marched with a rifle, either outside Bancroft or inside near the Battalion office, occasionally in Mitscher or in the Rotunda, for stipulated periods—usually in 45-minute increments. Sometimes a midshipman will be given a "room tour" in which he or she serves the tour in his or her room—studying. Tours are generally served for minor infractions, and following the marching of a tour a midshipman may go on liberty.

Restriction is different. Midshipmen on restriction (a) work off demerits during periods of restriction, and (b) report for muster several times a day in inspection-ready uniform. They may not leave their Company area except for classes and athletics, and they certainly may not go on liberty or even depart The Yard. And if their restriction period extends into or through a leave period (vacation), upperclassmen will remain at the Academy during some or all of their leave.

The Academy has a Table of Authorized Punishment, wherein various "fry-able" offenses are accorded points in increments of

1,000; each number of points then translates into a designated duration of restriction. The mildest offenses are in the 1,000-range; the worst are 6,000.

Among 5,000-series offenses:

—Violation of orders
—Failure to perform a duty, or interfering with another's performance of a duty
—Aiding in a 4,000-series (or higher) offense
—Abuse of the Plebe Indoctrination system
—Destruction of documents
—Disrespect or insubordination
—Fraternization
—Sexual harassment (mild)
—Fleeing the police
—Drinking (underage or mild)
—Destruction of government property (less than $500)
—Losing a weapon or handling it carelessly
—Unauthorized absence (less than 24 hours, intentional)

Among 6,000-series offenses (with strong potential for separation):

—Repeated hazing
—Marriage
—Sexual misconduct or sexual harassment (major)
—Repeated fraternization
—Drinking (repeated or major)
—Drunk driving
—Possession or use of drugs
—Conviction of a felony
—Destruction of government property (more than $500)
—Unauthorized absence (more than 24 hours)

There are lesser punishments. All are factored into a midshipman's conduct grade and remain on his or her record (in his or her "jacket") until graduation.

SEPARATION

It means leaving the Academy and takes one of two basic forms: voluntary resignation or involuntary discharge.

If voluntary, a midshipman usually separates because of unhappiness or incompatibility—the Academy experience proving to be something other than what he or she had expected. A midshipman might also voluntarily resign if he or she faces the prospect of dismissal for reasons of academics or discipline.

Plebes may not resign before they have spent 30 days at the Academy following Induction.

Midshipmen who separate in their Plebe or Youngster year ordinarily face no subsequent obligation of military service, although they will have to pay off all expenses and loans.

Midshipmen who separate after the beginning of classes for their Second Class year but before the beginning of their First Class year may be asked to reimburse the Academy and/or to serve as enlisted sailors in the fleet for up to two years.

Midshipmen who separate after the beginning of classes for their First Class year may be asked to reimburse the Academy and/or to serve as enlisted sailors in the fleet for up to three years.

Reimbursement—an Academy calculation based on equivalent amounts for a separating midshipman's supplies, room, board, teachers' salaries, etc.—can prove to be a big number, approaching $100,000.

The United States Code governs the separation process. The Secretary of the Navy must approve all Academy separations—voluntary or involuntary, for academic or disciplinary reasons.

SUMMER TRAINING

All midshipmen participate in Summer Training—both to learn more about the Navy and Marines and to learn about their career options.

It begins, really, with Plebe Summer. Once inducted (usually the first week of July), Plebes endure the rigors until Parents Weekend in August.

Thereafter, the guideline is this: Of three one-month "blocks" every summer, upperclassmen serve two—or 8 weeks of the 12.

Depending on their class standing, on what they request, and on the vagaries of scheduling, they might serve the first two blocks, the last two, or the first and last. The block in which they do not do summer training is available for summer leave—unless they (a) choose another summer-training elective, or (b) choose to (or have to) attend summer school.

Summer training looks like this:

> Rising Youngsters serve three weeks on a YP (Yard Patrol craft); then some serve three weeks on a sailboat, while the others serve three weeks at the Academy in naval tactical training—consisting of small-unit and joint-familiarization programs.
>
> Rising Second Class serve four weeks on a gray-hull cruise, learning about shipboard life and sharing the tasks of top-ranked enlisteds; some serve on Plebe Detail, training Plebes at the Academy; others have week-long samplings of life (a) as a pilot at Pensacola, (b) as a submariner at Kings Bay, Georgia, and (c) as a Marine at The Basic School in Quantico, Virginia.
>
> Rising First Class serve four to eight weeks aboard a fleet ship or submarine if they are not considering the Marines or SEALs; life is lived as junior officers. Marine and SEAL prospects may do either Leatherneck and the Fleet Marine Force (FMF) or Mini-BUD/S, respectively. Some Firsties do Plebe Detail, training Plebes at the Academy.

Among electives offered to midshipmen for summer training: foreign exchange (summer cruise with a foreign navy), language training abroad, internships, jump school, dive school, and SERE (survival, evasion, resistance, and escape) school.

LIBERTY AND LEAVE

Leave is the longer variety, for such things as summer, Thanksgiving, Christmas, and spring vacations.

Liberty is the shorter, usually no more than 96 hours. It comes in three basic forms: Yard liberty, town liberty, and weekend liberty.

Yard liberty is the freedom to go most places on the Academy campus. Generally, all midshipmen have it from 5:30 A.M. until taps.

Town liberty is the freedom to visit Annapolis and its immediate environs. It changes periodically, but at this writing generally:

—Firsties have it Monday, Tuesday, Thursday, and Friday (unless they are deficient in academics, conduct, or PE) from 4:00 P.M. (or following their last military obligation, whichever is later) until 10:00 P.M.; on Saturday they have it from the 10:15 A.M. liberty formation until 1:00 A.M. Sunday; on Sunday they have it until 6:00 P.M.; on Wednesday they have no town liberty.

—Second Class have it on Tuesday from 4:00 P.M. until 10:00 P.M. if they have an A in both conduct and performance, and if they are satisfactory in academics and PE; otherwise, on Saturday and Sunday they have it when Firsties have it.

—Third Class have it on Saturday and Sunday when Firsties have it.

—Plebes have it on Saturday when Firsties have it; otherwise, Plebes have no town liberty.

Weekend liberty is for those not deficient in academics, physical education, conduct, or performance. Generally:

—Firsties have an unlimited number of weekends, consistent with their obligations.

—Second Class have six per semester.

—Third Class have three per semester.

—Plebes have none unless authorized.

Midshipmen with particularly strong academic and military performance, notably those on the Superintendent's and Commandant's lists, may receive additional weekend liberty. Upperclassmen who are academically unsatisfactory generally receive one "unsat weekend" per semester.

What's more, though subject to change, these guidelines apply as of this writing:

—Firsties, Second Class, and Youngsters may leave for weekends only after the 10:15 A.M. liberty formation on Saturday and must return by 6:00 P.M. on Sunday.

BRIEF POINTS

Accountability—The term has numerous uses at the Naval Academy; one has to do with not being absent from or tardy to class; another has to do with responsibility—the importance placed on midshipmen developing it; assuming responsibility (or leadership) and taking responsibility for one's actions. Midshipmen and officers may delegate authority, but they are always accountable for their actions and the actions of those under them.

Enlisted Advisers—Senior noncommissioned officers (Navy master chief petty officers and Marine sergeants major) who serve at the Academy to advise and counsel midshipmen in how to lead enlistees. They serve as ombudsmen, assist Company Officers, and provide an enlisted perspective to soon-to-be officers.

Saluting—Incorporated into Navy regulations in 1893, the salute has an elusive history. One theory of its origin holds that in earlier times, when it was common to kill by dagger, individuals meeting one another often approached with their hands raised and their palms facing out to show they contained no concealed weapon. The Plebe manual *Reef Points* adds: The salute "is centuries old, and probably originated when men in armor raised their helmet visors so they could be identified. Salutes are customarily given with the right hand, but there are exceptions. A sailor with his right arm or hand encumbered may salute left-handed, while people in the [Marines,] Army[,] or Air Force never salute left-handed. On the other hand, a soldier or airman may salute sitting down or uncovered (without cap on); in the Navy, a sailor does not salute when uncovered (unless failure to do so would mean embarrassment or misunderstanding), but may salute when seated in a vehicle. Women in the Navy follow the same customs and rules as men in saluting, with one exception. A woman in uniform indoors, where men customarily remove their hats, does not remove her hat, nor does she salute....[Midshipmen should] salute all officers, men and women, of all U.S. services and all allied foreign services. Officers in the U.S. Merchant Marine and Public Health Service wear uniforms that closely resemble Navy uniforms, and they too rate a salute. There is one simple rule of saluting: When in doubt, salute."

Visitation—Visits to midshipmen's rooms in Bancroft are not ordinarily permitted except on two occasions: (1) during Plebe Parents Weekend at the end of Plebe Summer, and (2) during Firstie Parents Weekend in First Class year (usually September). The Command Duty Officer may authorize room visits by parents and guardians at other times. Visits to King Hall for lunch or dinner are routine for upperclass hosts, assuming the host midshipman acquires appropriate meal tickets ahead of time.

BRIEFER POINTS

For a full definition of the following terms, see the glossary.

All-Calls	BOOW	CMEO (pronounced
Alpha Code	Brace Up (verb)	*simeo*)
Article	Brag Sheet	CMOD (pronounced
ASTB	Brassard	*see-mod*)
Basket Leave	Brick	Color Company
Batt-O	Capstone	Color Girl
Battalion Officer	Carry-On	Color Parade
(Batt Officer)	CDO	Colors
Bed Check	Chain of Command	Come-Around
Billet	Chit	Company
Black Monday	Chopping	Company
(or Sunday)	Chow Calls	Commander
Black N	Cinderella Libs	Company Officer
Board	Civvies	Company Wardroom
BOM	Classmate Loyalty	Conduct

The Countdown
Cover
CSORM (pronounced *see-sorm*)
The Days
Dead Week
Demerits
Dining In
Dining Out
Drill
Duty Section
EI
EMI
End of Semester Leave
Evolution
Extra Duty
Eyes in the Boat
First Class Cruise
Flamer
Formation
Form 2
Fraternization
Fry
Fry Trap
Gig Line
GOOB
Grab-and-Go
Grease
Hair
Height and Weight Restrictions
Honor Committee
Honor Concept
Indoc
Inspections

Intersessional
Jewelry
Late Lights
Leatherneck
Mess Night
Mid (Mids)
Middy (Middies)
MidRegs
Mini-BUD/S
Morning Quarters
MPSS
Muster
NASP
Officer's Call
On Duty
1/C
1-90 (pronounced *one tac 90*)
On Report
ORB
Order of Merit
Over the Wall
PCR
Performance
Performance Board
Plebe
Plebe Detail
Plebe Summer
Plebe Year
Pre-Commissioning Week
Pre-Comms
Professional Knowledge
Radius
Reef Points

Responses
Restriction
Reveille
Scramble (verb)
Service Assignment
Sets
Shotgun
Sir (Ma'am)
Sound Off
Squad
Squad Leader
Tables
Taps
Thanksgiving Rule
Tour
2 for 8
Two-Inch Bulk Rule
2% Club
UA
Using My Honor Against Me
Weekend Eligible
Wings

🔱 🔱 🔱 🔱 🔱 🔱 🔱 🔱

5 / ATHLETICS AND PHYSICAL TRAINING

The Academy requires four years of physical education and year-round athletics. Every season every midshipman must participate in a sport—either intercollegiate, intramural, or club. For the most part, those on varsity or junior varsity (jv) squads participate in or train for their sport year-round, and therefore are exempt from competition at intramural or club levels in what might be considered off-seasons.

For example: varsity and jv athletes do not ordinarily play intramural or club sports; nor do they ordinarily play on more than one varsity-level team. Midshipmen on in-season varsity and jv teams are also exempt from marching and parade drill (men's basketball is exempted out of season because its members stand watch as side boys at parades). Under NCAA guidelines, they are limited to 20 hours of team practice per week.

INTERCOLLEGIATE

The Academy offers competition in 21 intercollegiate varsity sports for men and in 9 for women; annually, Navy teams compete in about 550 intercollegiate contests. The 29 intercollegiate sports are:

Men:	**Women:**
Baseball	Basketball
Basketball	Crew
Crew (heavyweight)	Cross Country
Crew (lightweight)	Sailing
Cross Country	Soccer
Football	Swimming
Football (150-pound)	Track (indoor)
Golf	Track (outdoor)
Gymnastics	Volleyball
Lacrosse	
Rifle	
Sailing	
Soccer	
Squash	
Swimming	
Tennis	
Track (indoor)	
Track (outdoor)	
Volleyball	
Water Polo	
Wrestling	

The Academy offers junior varsity intercollegiate competition in 10 men's sports and in 2 women's sports. They are:

Men:	**Women:**
Baseball	Basketball
Basketball	Crew
Crew (heavyweight)	
Crew (lightweight)	
Football	
Golf	
Rifle	
Squash	
Tennis	
Wrestling	

Because jv squads are considered feeders for varsity squads, in almost no cases do midshipmen compete on jv squads beyond Youngster year. If they do not make varsity teams by Second Class year, they usually move to intramural or club competition.

Finally, the Academy offers interscholastic competition for Plebes in crew for both men and women.

INTRAMURAL

Intramural sports cover a broad range; some are played at the Company level, some at the Battalion level. Intramural teams practice or compete for about two hours three to five afternoons per week—when their members do not have military obligations; contrary to members of varsity, jv, and Plebe teams, members of intramural teams (like most members of out-of-season intercollegiate teams) are not exempt from drill. Coaches, managers, and referees are First Class and Second Class midshipmen. Managers oversee equipment and schedules.

Intramurals are coed except for fieldball and touch football, both of which are closed to women. Intramural sports at the Academy for the 1995–96 academic year were:

Fall:
    Basketball (five players against five)
    Soccer
    Touch Football
Winter:
    Basketball (three players against three)
    Fieldball
    Racquetball
    Weightlifting
Spring:
    Disc Football (Ultimate Frisbee)
    Softball
    Volleyball

CLUB

Club sports differ somewhat from intramurals. They begin as extra-curricular activities and must remain ECAs for four years, at which time they may be elevated to club status. (Currently several sports are ECAs and could become certified club sports.) Like intramural teams, club teams practice for about two hours three to five afternoons per week—when their members do not have military obligations; their members are not drill-exempt. Most club-level coaches are faculty volunteers. As intercollegiate teams do, club teams have an O Rep. Such teams arrange their own schedules and travel. They compete against similar teams at collegiate or post-collegiate levels.

Among club sports are:

Men:
> Boxing
> Ice Hockey
> Lacrosse
> Rugby
> Volleyball

Women:
> Gymnastics
> Soccer
> Softball
> Tennis

Coed:
> Bicycling
> Judo
> Karate
> Powerlifting

LEAGUES, CONFERENCES

The Naval Academy is a member of the National Collegiate Athletic Association (NCAA), the Eastern Collegiate Athletic Conference (ECAC), and the Patriot League. In the Patriot League it competes in baseball, men's and women's basketball, golf, soccer, tennis, women's swimming, and women's volleyball. In crew, it is a member of the Eastern Association of Rowing Colleges (EARC). Navy competes against Army 21 times per year.

ATHLETIC ASSOCIATION

The nonprofit Naval Academy Athletic Association (NAAA—often called the N-Triple-A) administers, promotes, and variously assists with the Academy's intercollegiate athletic programs. Ticket sales, television revenues, and private contributions are the NAAA's primary sources of money. It hires coaches and staffs for such sports as football and men's basketball. It provides equipment, arranges for travel and lodging, sets schedules, sells tickets, and handles contest details. It operates and maintains the football stadium. And the NAAA runs the Naval Academy Visitor Center and the Tour Guide Service, whose earnings help fund special events and various Brigade activities. In addition, the NAAA assesses each midshipman about $44 annually as—in effect—an athletic activities fee for equipment, travel, and admission to all games.

FACILITIES

Among the Academy's major athletic facilities are

- —The 30,000-seat Navy–Marine Corps Memorial Stadium.
- —The 5,700-seat Alumni Hall.
- —The 6,217-yard golf course.
- —The Olympic-size Lejeune swimming pool with seating for 1,000, plus a lap tank (in Macdonough Hall), a diving well (Lejeune), and a pool for water polo (Macdonough).
- —The 5,000-seat Max Bishop baseball stadium.
- —A synthetic-surface field for football, soccer, and lacrosse.
- —A 400-meter all-weather outdoor track.
- —A 220-yard indoor track.
- —The Dahlgren indoor ice-hockey rink.
- —A wrestling room, weight-training and personal-conditioning rooms, gymnastics areas, boxing rings, shooting ranges, about 75 acres of lighted fields, 10 basketball courts, 50 rowing shells (33 eight-seat, 10 four-seat, 3 two-seat, and 4 one-seat), 30 tennis courts, and 15 squash courts.

SAILING

In conjunction with the NAAA, the Naval Academy Sailing Squadron—housed with the Sailing Department and the Naval Academy Sailing Foundation in the Robert Crown Sailing Center—oversees the Academy's competitive sailing program. The Academy's resources afloat include about 200 craft—from 20 108-foot YPs maintained at the Naval Station, to Lasers and Rainbows, sloops and yawls, and 90 sailboards.

O REPS AND FAC REPS

Midshipmen on most varsity, jv, Plebe, and club teams have Officer Representatives, called O Reps; some have Faculty Representatives, called Fac Reps.

O Reps, who are active-duty officers, must be approved annually. They work for the Commandant and for the Athletic Director. They serve both as role models for team members and as links between the teams and the administration. They assist with finances for the teams, help arrange for their transportation, and accompany the teams on away engagements.

Fac Reps, who are full-time members of the Academy faculty, track the academic performance of team members and assist—as necessary—with such things as setting up extra instruction. Sometimes they travel with the teams.

TABLES

Athletes on in-season teams, or on teams with year-round commitments, frequently eat with their teammates at Team Tables (as opposed to the regular Squad Tables) in King Hall. In accordance with NCAA rules, athletes at such tables receive no special food.

LETTERS

Letters, or Ns, are earned by athletes participating in intercollegiate sports. For the most part, varsity Ns are awarded to midshipmen who have played a stipulated minimum of the time that their team competed during its season. An N* (N-star) is awarded to those letter-winners whose team defeats Army in the annual competition. About 460 men and 140 women win varsity Ns during an academic year. Those lettering for three years may be awarded, as Firsties, either an N blanket or a watch by the NAAA.

In addition, team and Plebe Ns may be awarded to midshipmen on varsity, jv, or Plebe teams who do not qualify for varsity Ns. There are also Ns for varsity, jv, and Plebe managers and assistant managers. And letters, with the specific sport designated, are awarded in club sports.

PHYSICAL TRAINING

Every midshipman receives instruction in certain sports. In addition, every midshipman must satisfy certain physical-education requirements.

> —All Plebes receive instruction—and grades—in swimming, weight training, and lifetime fitness.
> —All Youngsters receive instruction—and grades—in swimming, judo, boxing, and/or combative grappling.
> —All Second Class receive instruction—and grades—in swimming and hand-to-hand combat.
> —All Firsties receive instruction—and grades—in lifetime fitness.

Second Class and Firsties must also choose from these electives: badminton, baseball, diving, first aid, golf, kayaking, pistol/rifle, racquetball, squash, tennis, and volleyball.

In addition to regular physical-education classes and annual swimming tests, there's the semester mile-and-a-half run. To pass, men must run it in a maximum of 10 minutes 30 seconds, women in a maximum of 12 minutes 40 seconds. There's also the semester Physical Readiness Test (PRT)—consisting of push-ups, sit-ups, and the sit-and-reach flexibility test (one sits with one's legs flat on the floor and touches one's toes).

Different PRT standards apply to each gender. The minimums are

> Men:
> 40 push-ups in two minutes
> 65 sit-ups in two minutes
> pass sit-and-reach

Women:
    18 push-ups in two minutes
    65 sit-ups in two minutes
    pass sit-and-reach

Better performance earns better grades. Those "validating" for the next semester, thereby to avoid taking the PRT in that semester, must earn grades of at least 90 percent.

Midshipmen not meeting the requirements (that is, those judged "PE deficient") are placed on sub squads (for swimming), conditioning squads (for PRT), and remedial squads until they do. Failure likely will result in loss of leave. Those failing repeatedly likely will be put on probation or sent to the Academic Board for further review.

BRIEFER POINTS
For a full definition of the following terms, see the glossary.

Conditioning Squad	NASS
Fall Ball	PE Deficient
Fieldball	PEP
40-Year Swim	Physical Readiness Test (PRT)
Grappling	Pre-Test
Halsey Hack	Reg PE Gear
Hand to Gland	The Rocks
Inner (or Outer)	Sub Squad
Marlinspike Seamanship	Team Tables
Mile-and-a-Half	10-Meter Board
Misery Hall	Validate

6 / **MONEY**

General Accounting Office calculations for the dollar value of a four-year Academy education range in the $200,000 neighborhood per midshipman.

PAY

What's more, midshipmen receive about $558 per month, or about $6,700 per year—a figure that periodically goes up. Midshipmen and their families pay nothing for tuition, room, and board. Nor do they pay anything for medical and dental care.

Monthly net pay is of course less than the $558 gross—and considerably so in Plebe and Youngster years: the Academy deducts numerous costs from midshipmen's pay, with the bulk of deductions for big-ticket items such as uniforms and computers (which, contrary to widespread belief, are not free) coming up front in the early part of the Academy experience.

Except before major vacations, midshipmen generally receive their pay through direct deposit to a bank of their choice (almost always the Navy Federal Credit Union, NFCU) on the last working day of each month. They also receive a monthly Midshipmen Pay

	JUL	AUG	SEP	OCT	NOV
INCOME					
1 balance brought FWD	*774.00*	*886.30*	*412.10*	*391.90*	*504.20*
2 Pay	*558.04*	*558.04*	*558.04*	*558.04*	*558.04*
3 Comrats			*142.50*		
Total income	*1332.04*	*1444.34*	*1112.64*	*949.94*	*1062.24*
FIXED EXPENSES					
4 FITW	*20.05*	*20.05*	*20.05*	*20.05*	*20.05*
5 FICA	*42.69*	*42.69*	*42.69*	*42.69*	*42.69*
6 SITW	*13.00*	*13.00*	*13.00*	*13.00*	*13.00*
7 SGLI	*9.00*	*9.00*	*9.00*	*9.00*	*9.00*
8 Laundry & Services	*76.00*	*76.00*	*76.00*	*76.00*	*76.00*
Total Fixed Expenses	*160.74*	*160.74*	*160.74*	*160.74*	*160.74*
VARIABLE EXPENSES					
9 Store Issue		60.00	65.00		
10 Contract Tailor					
11 Books		340.00			
12 School Supplies		20.00			
13 Uniform Replacement		30.00			
14 Midstore Charges					
15 Publications		14.00	55.00		
16 Midshipmen Activities		22.50	55.00		
17 Misc. Auth. Charges					
18 Class Unique Items		100.00	100.00		61.50
19 Alumni Assoc.					
20 Cash Pay	170.00	170.00	170.00	170.00	170.00
21 Govt Loan Repay	115.00	115.00	115.00	115.00	115.00
Total Variable Expenses	285.00	871.50	560.00	285.00	346.50
22 MIDN Account Balance	886.30	412.10	391.90	504.20	555.00
23 Loan Balance	1360.00	1245.00	1130.00	1015.00	900.00

Sample pages from a "Midshipman Annual Budget" for a male Second Class
in the class of 1997. Net pay appears on line 20.

	DEC	JAN	FEB	MAR	APR	MAY	JUN	TOTAL CURRENT YEAR
	555.00	637.30	449.24	356.33	187.63	101.21	148.51	
	558.04	558.04	558.04	558.04	558.04	558.04	558.04	6696.48
		19.64	93.29		39.28			294.71
	1113.04	1214.98	1100.57	914.37	784.95	659.25	706.55	6991.19
	20.05	20.05	20.05	20.05	20.05	20.05	20.05	240.60
	42.69	42.69	42.69	42.69	42.69	42.69	42.69	512.28
	13.00	13.00	13.00	13.00	13.00	13.00	13.00	156.00
	9.00	9.00	9.00	9.00	9.00	9.00	9.00	108.00
	76.00	76.00	76.00	76.00	76.00	76.00	76.00	912.00
	160.74	160.74	160.74	160.74	160.74	160.74	160.74	1928.88
					73.00			198.00
			236.00	146.00				382.00
		260.00						600.00
		20.00						40.00
		30.00						60.00
								0.00
								69.00
			22.50					100.00
		10.00	10.00	10.00	15.00	15.00	15.00	75.00
			125.00	100.00				486.50
				50.00	50.00	50.00		150.00
	200.00	170.00	200.00	170.00	170.00	170.00	170.00	2100.00
	115.00	115.00	115.00	115.00	115.00	115.00	115.00	1380.00
	315.00	605.00	583.50	566.00	523.00	350.00	350.00	5640.50
	637.30	449.24	356.33	187.63	101.21	148.51	195.81	
	785.00	670.00	555.00	440.00	325.00	210.00	95.00	

U. S. NAVAL ACADEMY
MIDSHIPMEN PAY STATEMENT

I D	NAME		ALPHA	COMPANY 02	PERIOD COVERED 05/31/95

EARNINGS

COM RATS		42.75
PAY		558.04
	TOTAL EARNINGS	600.79

DEDUCTIONS

FEDERAL TAX	16.50
FICA TAX	42.69
SGLI	9.00
LAUNDRY	50.50
PERSONAL SERVICES	25.50
ACE REPAYMENT	125.00
ALUMNI ASSOCIATION	50.00
NAVY RELIEF	20.00
PLEBE DETAIL SHIRTS	30.00
TOTAL DEDUCTIONS	369.19

PAYMENTS SINCE LAST MPS :
05/31/95   200.00

PREVIOUS BALANCE $1071.61
ENDING BALANCE $1103.21

BASED ON CURRENT INFORMATION, YOUR NEXT MONTH'S
PAY IS EXPECTED TO BE :   150.00

REMARKS :

B A L	BALANCE FWD FM PREVIOUS MONTH 1071.61	TOTAL EARNINGS 600.79	TOTAL DEDUCTIONS 369.19	PAYMENTS SINCE LAST MPS 200.00	ENDING BALANCE 1103.21	DEBT TO GOVT (ACE BALANCE) 1600.00

T A X	EXEM S2	FED TAX PAID TO DATE 82.50	FICA TAX PAID TO DATE 213.45	STATE TAX PAID TO DATE .00	STATE CODE CA	PREVIOUS STATE CODE

NDW-USNA-BBA-7220/119   (7-90)

A sample "Midshipmen Pay Statement."

Statement (MPS). It lists withholding and deductions for everything from loan repayments and computer maintenance and textbooks, to Naval Academy Store purchases and uniforms and class fees.

A budget issued to every midshipman serves as a guide.

Net pay (midshipmen sometimes refer to their net pay as "the monthly insult") for Plebes is about $50 per month.

Net pay for Youngsters is about $150 per month for the entire year.

Second Class and First Class midshipmen are on a slightly different pay system that more closely reflects their individual charges. For the most part Second Class receive about $170 per month in net pay, and First Class about $300.

Upon entering the Academy, midshipmen or their families deposit about $2,000 with the Academy to offset the costs of books, computer, and uniforms. The government also lends all midshipmen $5,000 (an Additional Clothing and Equipment [ACE] loan) to cover the remainder of initial outfitting. To amortize the loan, the Academy makes deductions from each midshipman's pay during the first two years. Midshipmen separating prior to paying off the loan must repay the government in full. Midshipmen separating thereafter may also be required to pay certain amounts, perhaps totaling many thousands of dollars.

PERKS
Midshipmen also enjoy a number of financial perks. Among them:

- —The opportunity to sign up for telephone charge cards and for bank charge cards. Midshipmen annually receive offers for bank cards with some of the nation's lowest rates. Typically, the best offer comes from the Navy Federal Credit Union (NFCU) cash card or from the United Services Automobile Association (USAA) Visa and MasterCard.
- —The opportunity to open accounts or buy insurance at financial institutions such as NFCU and the Navy Mutual Aid Association. NFCU, which most midshipmen use for their checking and savings accounts, has an office in Bancroft.
- —Privileges at military commissaries and exchanges.

—Low-rate insurance, from group life to automobile (primarily USAA), to renter's (or tenant homeowner's), to personal property (primarily Armed Forces).
—Frequent discounts for commercial lodging and transportation.
—Space-available flights on military transport aircraft.

MEDICAL INSURANCE, ETC.

As members of the armed forces, midshipmen are automatically covered for all their medical and dental care. It is, in effect, free. The Navy provides or pays for all reasonable medical and dental expenses that a midshipman may incur—including emergency care received in civilian facilities.

In cases requiring long-term care, midshipmen are normally transferred to a military, Veterans Affairs, or civilian facility. When an injury or illness renders a midshipman not physically qualified for commissioning, the midshipman may be disenrolled—whereupon government financing of subsequent medical care may cease. Parental retention of medical insurance on their midshipmen may be a good idea during the years at the Academy.

What's more:

—Contrary to most others on active duty, disabled midshipmen do not qualify for military disability pay.
—The government likely will deny medical benefits in cases involving injury caused by a midshipman's willful misconduct or negligence—notably drinking.

FINANCIAL ADVISER

A Supply Corps officer serves as Midshipman Financial Adviser. Privately or via seminars, he or she assists midshipmen on subjects such as taxes, budgeting, insurance, savings, and loans—the Big Financial World. The adviser also serves as a source of forms and printed financial material.

LOANS

At the end of Second Class year, various financial institutions offer loans—called Career Starter Loans (widely known among midship-

marily class rank, medical status, and summer (or prior-enlistment) training. Those midshipmen who, for whatever reason, do not get their most coveted assignment (about 88 percent do) may be assigned to another community and then attempt a lateral transfer to their preferred community early in their career; such moves are difficult and never guaranteed, and—when successful—require several years of top performance in the community initially selected.

Standard paths are shown on pages 78 and 79.

SURFACE LINE

Basic Surface Warfare Officer School (SWOS) in Newport, Rhode Island (four months); then—for those in conventional propulsion—possibly a brief period in follow-on courses in (for example) engineering, weapons, or operations; then a first tour on a ship (chosen, along with home port and a class convening date, at Service Selection) for about 30 months.

Those selecting surface nuclear, on a carrier or a guided-missile cruiser, attend Nuclear Power School in Orlando, Florida, for six months, then train at a nuclear reactor prototype site for another six months, then attend a SWO school for four months, then serve a first tour on a ship; sometimes they attend a SWO school first, and then embark on the nuclear-training path. Nuclear-trained surface officers may command either conventional or nuclear ships, but officers lacking nuclear training may command only non-nuclear ships.

SUBMARINES

Only those admitted to nuclear power may select submarines. Following commissioning, they attend Nuclear Power School in Orlando, Florida (six months); then go to a nuclear reactor prototype site for six months (at Ballston Spa, New York, or Charleston, South Carolina); then attend Navy Submarine School (the submarine counterpart of SWO school) in New London, Connecticut (12 weeks); then serve a first tour of about 36 months on a nuclear attack, ballistic-missile (boomer), or Trident submarine. At Service Assignment, those going to subs do not choose the submarine in which they will first serve.

	1992 MALE	1992 FEMALE	1993 MALE	1993 FEMALE	1994 MALE	1994 FEMALE	1995 MALE	1995 FEMALE
USMC GROUND	100	3	129	7	114	11	74	8
USMC PILOT	33	0	50	0	48	2	29	1
USMC NFO	5	0	5	0	5	0	5	0
SURFACE								
(CONV)	273	10	248	14	277	52	178	40
(OCEAN)	3	1	7	1	4	3	3	5
(ED)	0	0	0	0	6	0	7	2
(NUC)	19	0	16	0	22	6	34	3
SUBS	92	**	102	**	90	**	87	**
SPEC WAR	10	**	16	**	16	**	16	**
SPEC OPNS	9	1	8	1	10	0	7	1
NFO	109	5	105	3	53	3	89	11
PILOT	216	14	203	12	135	10	197	12
AMD	0	0	0	1	0	1	0	3
CRYPTOLOGY	1	2	3	1	2	0	2	2
INTELLIGENCE	3	2	3	2	5	4	7	5
OCEANOGRAPHY	0	1	0	1	2	0	0	2
MED CORPS	15	0	17	1	12	1	12	1
SUPPLY	19	13	17	13	19	5	31	6
CEC	4	6	5	4	8	0	6	1
USAF	5	2	12	1	1	2	5	1
USA	0	0	2	0	2	0	1	0
GEN URL	6	34	11	30	*	*	*	*

*NO LONGER AVAILABLE   **NOT AVAILABLE TO FEMALES

USNA Service Assignment for the classes of 1992, 1993, 1994, and 1995.

NAVAL AVIATION

While at the Naval Academy, midshipmen who want to fly must be physically qualified (with color-vision proficiency and 20/30 uncorrected eyesight) and must pass a two-part, three-hour exam (the Aviation Standard Test Battery [ASTB]). A test and predictor similar to the Scholastic Aptitude Test (SAT), the ASTB measures (a) aptitude for flight-school academics, (b) aptitude for flying, and (c) biographical inventory. Midshipmen failing the test must wait 30 days before trying again. (Although the medical standards for Navy and Marine pilots and NFOs are practically the same, the Marines do have slightly more stringent standards on the ASTB exam.)

Naval Flight Officers (NFOs) must also meet all the standards a pilot must meet except the standards for uncorrected eyesight and color acuity.

At Service Assignment, midshipmen going air do not pick a specific type of aircraft; rather, their equivalent of a SWO's choice of a ship is a flight-training class date for aviation training. The choice of aircraft to be flown during one's career comes at the completion of initial flight training.

Those with air billets go first to aviation indoctrination (or ground) school in Pensacola, Florida, followed by a 22-week primary training that ends with the awarding of wings. (To this point, Navy and Marine aviators receive exactly the same training, hence all are naval aviators.) Then, depending on the type of aircraft they will fly, pilots either stay in Pensacola (jets and helicopters) or go to Kingsville, Texas (jets), Meridian, Mississippi (jets), or Corpus Christi, Texas (propeller aircraft) for further training (about a year). NFOs, who are not pilots, remain in Pensacola. Total training time for pilots and NFOs—from the beginning of ground school—is 18–24 months. They then report to a replacement squadron in the fleet.

SPECIAL WARFARE

Basic Underwater Demolition School (BUD/S) for SEALs in Coronado, California (six months); then junior officer school in Coronado (several weeks); then report to a team at either Coronado or Little Creek, Virginia, for a first tour of two or three years, during which time there is specialized training.

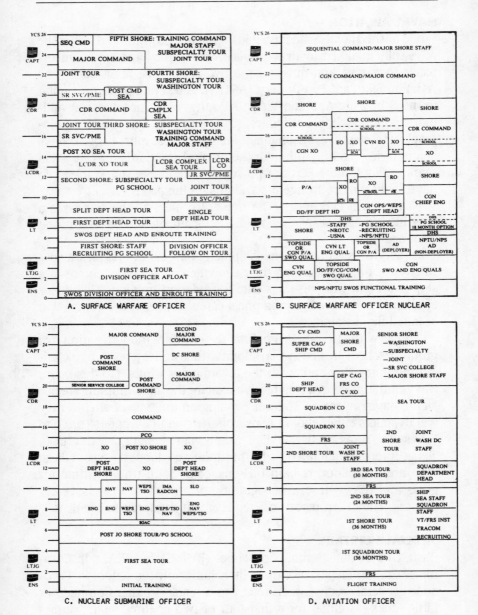

Typical career paths for naval officers
(from "Useful Information for Commissioned Officers").

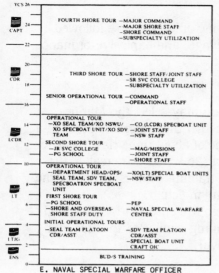

E. NAVAL SPECIAL WARFARE OFFICER

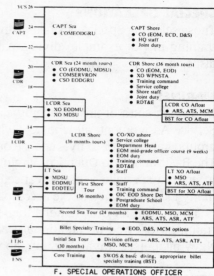

F. SPECIAL OPERATIONS OFFICER

G. GENERAL SUPPLY CORPS OFFICER

SPECIAL OPERATIONS

Those selecting Special Ops take a diving officers' course followed by training in (for example) diving, salvage, and explosive-ordnance disposal.

MARINES

Up to one-sixth of any Academy class may select the Marines. At Service Assignment, all who do—whether they intend to serve in a ground specialty or to fly—choose one of about three class dates for The Basic School in Quantico, Virginia (26 weeks). Thereafter, those in ground specialties take advanced training courses at one of the many locations listed in the accompanying chart.

Those with air designations then go to Pensacola for basic flight training, followed by additional training similar to that for many Navy pilots [see Naval Aviation, above].

OTHER

All midshipmen are commissioned as unrestricted line officers, with these exceptions: Those who become non-physically qualified (NPQ) prior to Service Assignment may be assigned intelligence, cryptology, aerospace maintenance, meteorology/oceanography (METOC), supply, or the construction engineering corps (CEC). In addition, 15 openings—or billets—in the medical corps are annually available to midshipmen.

MISCELLANY

> —Women are not assigned to submarines or the SEALs; all other Navy assignments are open to them—although in the Marines certain ground-combat assignments are not open to them.
> —Any Academy graduate who pursues government-funded graduate study incurs an additional service obligation— generally two additional years of active duty for each additional year of funded study at either a civilian university or at the Naval Postgraduate School in Monterey, California.
> —Up to 15 midshipmen may be selected each year for commissioning in the Army or Air Force.

OCCUPATIONAL FIELD	COURSE AND LOCATION	LENGTH
02 Ground Intelligence	Infantry Officer Course, The Basic School MCCDC, Quantico, VA	10 Weeks
	Military Intelligency Basic Course Fort Huachuca, AZ	18 Weeks
Aviation Intelligence	Naval Intelligence Basic Course Damneck, VA	18 Weeks
03 Infantry	Infantry Officer's Course The Basic School, MCCDC, Quantico, VA	8 Weeks
04 Logistics	Marine Integrated Maintenance Management Course LFTCLANT, Little Creek, VA	4 Weeks
08 Field Artillery	Field Artillery Officer Basic Course Fort Sill, OK	18.Weeks
13 Engineer	Combat Engineer Officer Course Marine Corps Service Support Schools MCB, Camp Lejeune, NC	7 Weeks
18 Tanks and Assault Amphibious Vehicle	Armor Officer Basic Course, Fort Knox, KY or	18 Weeks
	Assault Amphibian Vehicle, Officer Orientation Course MCB, Camp Pendleton, CA	9 Weeks
25 Communications	Basic Communications Officer's Course MCCDC, Quantico, VA	18 Weeks
26 Signal Intelligence/ Electronic Warfare	Basic Communications Officer's Course MCCDC, Quantico, VA	18 Weeks
	Naval Security Group Junior Officer's Orientations Course Pensacola, FL	9 Weeks
30 Ground Supply	Ground Supply Officer's Course MCB, Camp Lejeune, NC	12 Weeks
Aviation Supply	Marine Aviation Supply Officer's Course, Athens, GA	15 Weeks
34 Financial Management	Financial Management Officer's Course MCB, Camp Lejeune, NC	9 Weeks
35 Motor Transport	Motor Transport Officer's Course MCB Camp Lejeune, NC	7 Weeks
40 Data Systems	Data Systems Officer's Course, MCCDC, Quantico, VA	12 Weeks
43 Public Affairs	Information Officer's Course Ft. Benjamin Harrison, IN	10 Weeks
60 Aircraft Maintenance	Aircraft Maintenance Officer's Course Pensacola, FL	10 Weeks
72 Anti-air Warfare	Improved HAWK Officer's Course Fort Bliss, TX	10 Weeks
Air Support	Air Support Control Officer's Course Twentynine Palms, CA	11 Weeks
Air Defense	Air Defense Control Officer's Control Course Twentynine Palms, CA	20 Weeks
Air Traffic Control	Air Traffic Control Officer's Control Course Naval Air Technical Training Center, NAS Memphis, NAS, Memphis, Millington, TN	16 Weeks
75 Naval Flight Officer	Naval Flight Training Pensacola, FL	34 Weeks
Pilot	Naval Flight Training Pensacola, FL	Jets 75 Weeks Helicopters 60 Weeks

Military Occupational Specialty Schools for the Marines, with locations and durations (from "Marine Corps Update").

—Finally, in both the Navy and Marines the two- to three-year tours tend to alternate between ship and shore (or foreign and domestic) assignments.

OBLIGATION

All newly commissioned Navy ensigns or Marine second lieutenants (through the class of 1995) serve a minimum of five years of active duty, except: (1) Navy pilots serve seven years following receipt of their wings, and (2) Navy NFOs serve six years; (3) Marine pilots serve six to eight years following receipt of their wings, and (4) Marine NFOs serve six years.

The obligation is five years. Obligations for pilots and NFOs will remain the same for the class of 1996 as for those in earlier classes, until and unless changed by Congress. In addition, beginning with the class of 1997, Academy graduates will receive reserve commissions.

Temporary Additional Duty (TAD)—that is, duty new Academy graduates often serve while awaiting the beginning of their warfare school—does not add to service obligations. But it does extend the period of total service for those in aviation, because their years of obligation do not begin until receipt of their wings.

PAY AND INCENTIVES

For 1995, monthly base pay for new ensigns and second lieutenants with less than two years of service was $1,636. Ordinarily, young officers receive a promotion to the next rank within two years. (1995 monthly base pay for lieutenant jg's and first lieutenants was $2,058 for those with more than two years of service, and $2,473 for those with more than three years of service.)

In addition to the $1,636, they received about $146 a month for food and about $328 a month for housing (more if married). And to attract and retain young officers, there were these monthly monetary incentives for new ensigns and second lieutenants (incentives that, for the most part, increase with rank and years of service):

—$175 in submarine pay.
—$125 in flight pay.

—$110 in hazardous-duty pay (parachuting and diving).
—$150 in peacetime hostile-fire pay.

Plus:

—A $6,000 one-time incentive for those in nuclear power ($4,000 payable upon acceptance into the nuclear-power program, and the remaining $2,000 payable upon completion of nuclear-power training), plus an annual incentive of $10,000 per year.
—A $9,000 to $12,000 annual aviation incentive, payable upon completion of one's initial active-duty obligation; the amount changes annually, according to the needs of the Navy.

Finally, for surface officers, sea pay of $150 a month begins in the fourth year of accumulated sea duty, and it goes higher thereafter.

BREAST INSIGNIA

Most junior officers do not earn the right to wear their warfare-qualification breast insignia, or pin (or device), until a year or two after the completion of their post-Academy specialty schooling. For the most part, such pins are marks of both completed training and demonstrated proficiency within a warfare specialty—and are not awarded until one has served on a ship, submarine, or team, etc.

An exception is the aviation device, or wings—awarded upon completion of flight training. It indicates primarily that an individual has completed formal undergraduate pilot training. Following receipt of their wings, pilots and NFOs go to a training squadron, where they usually face another year of training in the type and model of aircraft they will fly in the fleet. After this they report to a fleet squadron.

WASHING OUT

Anyone washing out of specialty training—such as nuclear, air, or SEALs—continues service in whatever other part of the Navy or Marine Corps that may be assigned.

BRIEFER POINTS

For a full definition of the following terms, see the glossary.

Affirmative
Airdale
Another Great
    Navy Day
Another Great
    Navy Deal
ARRUGAH!
ASAP
AWOL
Backseater
The Basic School
Basket Leave
Best Orders
Billet
Blackshoe
Blood Pins
Bravo Zulu
Brownshoe
Bubblehead
BUD/S
Budweiser
Butter Bar
Cake-Eater
Career Path
Check Six
Chest Candy
Cryppie
Defense
    Language
    Institute (DLI)
Detailer
DOR
Duty Station
Fair Winds and
    Following Seas

Five and Dive
The Fleet
Flyboy
FMF
Four Years Together
    by the Bay
Fraternization
Ground Pounder
Haze Gray and
    Under Way
Head
High and Tight
HOO-YAH!
Intel
Jarhead
Jet Jockey
Leatherneck
Line Officer
Mameluke
Marine
Monterey
NAMI
Naval
The Naval Service
Negative
Negatory
NFO
Ninth Wing
Nuke
Obligation
OO-RAH!
Pentagram
Pipeline
Platform
PQ (or NPQ)

Pre-Comms
Prior
Puddle Pirate
Puzzle Palace
Reefer
Ring Knocker
Roger
Sandblower
SEAL
Service Assignment
The Silent Service
SIR
Skivvy Waver
Snake-Eater
SOP (pronounced
    ess-oh-pee)
Spawning Ground
    of the Navy
Spook
SPUDS
Station
Swarrior
SWO
SWO-Daddy
SWOS
TAD (pronounced
    tee-a-dee)
Tour
Water Wings
Wingman

♒ ♒ ♒ ♒ ♒ ♒ ♒

8 / **ODDS AND ENDS**

A good deal about the Naval Academy does not fit neatly into any category. Herewith, an alphabetical rundown of a diverse list of topics.[*]

ACADEMY ORGANIZATION
Who's on first?

Numero Uno at the Naval Academy, the equivalent of a civilian college president, is the Superintendent—selected for the post by the Chief of Naval Operations. (John Ryan, the incumbent Superintendent, is the 56th; most superintendents serve a two- or three-year term.)

The Superintendent (midshipmen call him the Supe) is usually a two-star unrestricted-line rear admiral (upper half) or a vice admiral. He directs the entire Academy operation, as well as the Annapolis area naval complex, oversees a more than $100-million annual Academy budget, and reports to the Chief of Naval Operations and the Secretary of the Navy (who reports to the Secretary of Defense, who reports to the Commander-in-Chief—the President).

[*] Note that the addresses and telephone numbers in this chapter may be subject to change.

By law, the Academy's oversight body is the Board of Visitors, which meets several times a year. Its members are appointed by Congress and the President. Those appointed by Congress are members of the Senate and the House of Representatives.

The Superintendent has six major assistants. Of them, the two most notable are:

—The Commandant of Midshipmen (midshipmen call him the Dant)—the midshipmen's commanding officer (there have been about 76). A senior captain or a one-star rear admiral, the Commandant is selected by the Superintendent and has duties that partly approximate those of a civilian college dean of students. In addition, as commander of the Brigade, the Commandant oversees discipline and military training. The Commandant probably has more direct effect on the daily lives of midshipmen than the Superintendent does.

—The Academic Dean and Provost, currently William C. Miller. He presides over the curriculum and the 600-member faculty and serves as the Superintendent's top academic counselor.

In addition, the Superintendent receives input from two permanent boards—the Board of Visitors and the Objectives Review Board (ORB). Perhaps foremost is the ORB, where he is joined by the Commandant, the Academic Dean, the directors of the four academic divisions, and other key officials. The ORB meets regularly to consider major matters of policy, but it has an unlimited charter. Although in session for only a few days per year, another board has particular importance, and holds particular dread, for midshipmen: the Academic Board. It considers the fate of midshipmen who have met the criteria for separation and determines whether they will leave or be retained.

ADDRESS

Many midshipmen practically *live* for mail. The Bancroft Post Office handles more than a ton of mail daily.

Anyone writing to a midshipman should know the addressee's class (or year of graduation) and Company (or Plebe Summer Platoon), as in these examples.

During Plebe Summer, the form for addressing mail is:

> Midshipman Adair Doe, '99
> Third Platoon
> U.S. Naval Academy
> Annapolis, Maryland 21412-5199

For all other midshipmen at all other times, the form for addressing mail is:

> Midshipman Adair Doe, '99
> Third Company
> U.S. Naval Academy
> Annapolis, Maryland 21412-5103
> (Note: the last two digits should conform to the
> midshipman's Company)

The zip code for mail addressed to anyone living or working in Bancroft (except the Commandant) is 21412. The zip code for mail addressed to anyone living or working elsewhere on The Yard is 21402. And Annapolis has several zip codes.

ADMISSIONS

The standards are high, the hopes and hoops are many, and those chosen are few. A midshipman profile appears elsewhere in these pages.

The Naval Academy is a hugely remarkable, commendable place. But it is different—offering a "collegiate" experience vastly different from those offered by civilian colleges. Prospective applicants should enter the admissions process only if they are relatively certain the Naval Academy is what they really want. Following induction, that decision will be questioned many times.

Many routes lead to admission. Nearly all applicants require two parts of an admissions ticket: (1) *approval by the Academy's*

Admissions Board, and (2) a *nomination* by (usually) a Senator or Congressman—none of whom may have more than five incumbent appointees at the Naval Academy (plus five at the Air Force Academy, plus five at West Point) at any time.

Some applicants receive approval by the Admissions Board but do not receive a politician's nomination. Many receive a politician's nomination but do not receive approval by the Admissions Board. (Politicians usually nominate ten applicants for each vacancy; except when a politician makes one of his ten a "principal" nominee, the Academy usually picks the nominees it wants from the pool of qualified nominees and alternates.) Only with both halves of the ticket in hand can the applicant hope to redeem them, in effect, for final Academy approval—an offer of an *appointment.*

The Academy has what amounts to a rolling admissions process. Those who submit their completed applications and related material early may hear early—at least regarding their disposition by the Admissions Board. The Academy begins in October offering appointments and letters of assurance—letters guaranteeing applicants' appointments upon their receipt of a politician's nomination; the Academy completes the process by mid-May.

See *Blue and Gold Officers* [below].

ALCOHOL

See *Drugs and Alcohol* [below].

ALUMNI ASSOCIATION

The official name of this private, independent, and nonprofit organization is the United States Naval Academy Alumni Association. Today's Alumni House is the former Ogle Hall, a pre-Revolutionary (1739) building two blocks from Gate 3—at the corner of King George Street and College Avenue.

The Alumni Association has nearly 35,000 members who—through it—keep up with the Academy and support it.

The association is a big operation. It keeps records on all who have taken the oath of office as midshipmen since 1845. It publishes an annual Register of Alumni and—10 times a year—an alumni-oriented magazine called *Shipmate.* It assists prospective applicants. It raises money for a broad range of tangible and intangible Academy needs not covered by federal funds—needs designated by the Superintendent; recently, for example, it raised half the cost of Alumni Hall through private funds. And it coordinates (and often provides speakers for) all other organizations, including parents' clubs, that support the Academy in various ways.

Address: 247 King George Street
           Annapolis, MD 21402-5068
           Phone: 410-263-4448 (Annapolis)
           410-269-1036 (Baltimore)
           410-261-2684 (Washington, D.C.)

ANNAPOLIS
Then....

The story goes that the town adjacent to the Naval Academy was founded in 1649 by 10 Puritan families driven out of Virginia by intolerant Anglicans. The Virginians named their settlement Providence. Over the years, it briefly took other names, such as the Town at Proctor's and Town of Severn. In 1670, the residents formally gave it the name Anne Arundel Town.

In 1695 the name changed again, to Annapolis—after James II's second daughter, Princess Anne, who later would become Queen; a year earlier Annapolis had replaced St. Mary's City as the capital of the Maryland colony. And in 1708 the newly laid out city near the confluence of the Chesapeake Bay and the Severn River received a royal charter of incorporation.

Few cities can boast a more distinguished history.

King William's School, forerunner of St. John's College, was founded in 1696; St. John's is just down College Avenue and across King George Street from the Naval Academy. The Maryland *Gazette,* one of the nation's oldest surviving newspapers, first began publication in Annapolis in 1727. The city long served as a major port, principally for the export of tobacco.

Annapolitans staged their own 1774 "Tea Party" when they forced the October burning of the brig *Peggy Stewart* because its owner (Anthony Stewart) had paid British authorities a tax on its one-ton cargo of tea. Three of Maryland's four signers of the Declaration of Independence were closely connected with Annapolis:

Charles Carroll of Carrollton was born there; Samuel Chase and William Paca lived there. (Today the houses of all three are well preserved.)

George Washington visited often. Rochambeau and Lafayette camped there in 1781 with their French and Colonial troops. For 10 months beginning in November 1783, Annapolis served as the nation's capital. Washington resigned his commission as Commander-in-Chief there, and there the Continental Congress ratified the Treaty of Paris ending the Revolutionary War.

Built in the 1770s on State Circle, the State House is the oldest state capitol still in use; the Governor's Mansion is nearby. The Maryland General Assembly convenes for 90 days annually from mid-January to mid-April.

During the Civil War, Annapolis served as a major port and embarkation point for Union troops. Temporarily, the Academy moved to Newport, Rhode Island, and the Academy grounds were turned into an Army post headquartering (among others) Generals Butler, Burnside, and Grant.

And now....

Today downtown Annapolis is not only a National Historic Site full of outstanding Georgian and Colonial architecture (the Paca House, the Chase-Lloyd House, and the Hammond-Harwood House stand close to the Academy; the Charles Carroll of Carrollton House stands several blocks farther away). The city remains one of the few with a downtown area essentially unchanged since colonial times. As it has since its inception, Annapolis continues as a busy port—combining a working waterfront with thousands of craft, both power and sail.

Annapolis remains the capital of Maryland, as well as the seat of Anne Arundel County. It boasts 35,000 people, diverse and vibrant culture, numerous boutiques and galleries, extensive lodging, and hundreds of restaurants. It also boasts the Naval Academy. The city's dock is two blocks from Gate 1 (and five blocks from Gate 3).

Washington is 33 miles due west. Baltimore is 30 miles north. Maryland's rural Eastern Shore (with towns such as St. Michaels, Oxford, and Easton) lies a few miles east, across the Chesapeake Bay Bridge.

Midshipmen sometimes refer to Annapolis as "downtown" or "Crabtown," and to its residents as "townies" or "Crabs." The terms are affectionate: Annapolis has just about everything. Midshipmen know it would be hard to imagine a town with more charm—or with more hospitality for them.

See *Boat Shows* and *Tours* [below].

ARMY-NAVY GAME

It is the great collegiate football game of the year. Nearly all midshipmen and Army cadets are required to attend. The NAAA sells tickets to the game separately from season-ticket packages [see *Tickets,* below].

Most Army-Navy games are played in Philadelphia; some are played elsewhere.

Tentative dates for future Army-Navy games are

December 7, 1996
December 6, 1997
December 5, 1998
December 4, 1999
December 2, 2000
December 1, 2001
December 7, 2002

BLUE AND GOLD OFFICERS

Their official name is Naval Academy Information Officers. The Candidate Guidance Office coordinates a network of about 1,700 of them. Its phone: 410-293-4361.

They're friends of the Academy—usually alumni, Naval Reserve officers, or civilians—who provide information and assist prospective midshipmen in the admissions process. They also interview candidates for admission, submitting written reports for consideration by the Admissions Board. See *Admissions* [above].

BOAT SHOWS

Annapolis packs in many thousands annually for its boat shows.

In the fall, the Sailboat Show is usually held on Columbus Day weekend in October; the Powerboat Show is usually held one week later. Each fall show draws many thousands.

A spring show, for both sail and power, is often held in late April; it currently attracts about half the number attending either of the fall shows.

The shows can make for good times and for monumental traffic congestion—particularly when they coincide with Navy home football games, and particularly when those games are against Air Force.

CARE PACKAGES

Sure. And send them often, while keeping in mind that storage can be a problem.

Midshipmen frequently call them "chow packages." Put in what the midshipman will want or need. Do not put in what he or she is not supposed to have. Snacks and such, particularly for Plebes, are almost always welcome: brownies, cereal, crackers, chips, cookies, soups, and small containers of juice. So are quarters for the vending machines and pay telephones. For the most part, follow the midshipman's desires and requests.

A note: For ease of pickup by midshipmen, parcel post (U.S. Mail) is usually preferable to United Parcel Service (UPS)—and definitely preferable during Plebe Summer.

CARS, MOTORCYCLES, AND BICYCLES

(1) *Cars:*

Firsties may own and drive a car anywhere, including (with the appropriate decals) on The Yard—and park there.

Second Class may keep a car two miles (or farther) from the Academy. They may drive (a) anywhere beyond the two-mile limit, (b) within the two-mile limit when departing on or returning from authorized leaves, and (c) when in uniform drive to and from The Yard, and work on it, for certain Academy functions and during Ring Dance weekend.

Youngsters and Plebes may not keep a car anywhere near the Academy; nor may they drive one anywhere near it except when on leave. And according to regulations, Plebes "are authorized to ride in taxicabs or private automobiles when accompanied or driven by parents, guardians, USNA approved sponsors, staff or faculty members, or when escorting to a formal dance, play, or concert [on] The Yard. First Class or dependents of sponsors may drive [Plebes] directly to and from a sponsor's home."

As for car rentals: The Academy has no rules pertaining to them. But assuming midshipmen are of the age stipulated by a given rental company for rental of vehicles, they enjoy the same discounts as active-duty service people.

(2) *Motorcycles:*

Regulations stipulate that unless possessing permission from the Commandant, no midshipman may "own, operate, or ride a motorcycle, moped, or motor-driven bicycle."

(3) *Bicycles:*

Regulations also stipulate that no midshipman may own or operate a bicycle on The Yard "except in conjunction with an approved club or NAAA sport activity."

CEMETERY

It dates from the late 1860s. It contains about 5,000 burial sites and about 2,500 niches in the newer Columbarium.

Those eligible for burial and interment are essentially: (1) any military person on active duty at the Academy at the time of death, and (2) the stillborn and infant children (under seven years old) of those on active Academy duty; (3) flag-rank Academy graduates; (4) unremarried spouses of anyone buried there; and (5) anyone in the Navy or Marines whose spouse is buried there.

Remaining space is limited. Ultimate decisions may fall to the Superintendent or the Secretary of the Navy.

CHURCH

See *Worship* [below].

CLASS RINGS, PINS, ETC.

Each class, via committee, designs its own class crest during Plebe year. In the spring of that year, members of the class are offered the opportunity to buy class crest pins, charms, stick pins, tie tacks, tie bars, cuff links, and N guards (attachable to class pins by chain) for holders of varsity letters. Depending on the item and its gold content, costs range from $100 to $250. The items are first available in about May of each year, but they remain on sale at the Naval Academy Store and elsewhere for the next three years.

Class rings come later. Toward the end of Youngster year, the process of selection begins: size, fit, finish, gold content, type of stone or plug in the center, special designs—whatever. Cost ranges from several hundred dollars to several thousand, depending on many variables.

The rings are not available until the spring of Second Class year, and are not supposed to be worn until the Ring Dance in late May. At that dance, the ring is dipped into a binnacle containing water from the seven seas. Tradition holds that the ring's Academy seal is worn facing outward and the class crest facing inward until Commissioning—when the ring is turned around and the sides thus reversed. Class rings are made in miniature versions for giving as engagement rings. Women midshipmen may order the miniature in lieu of the larger class ring.

Regulations stipulate that any midshipman not graduating and receiving a diploma, "for any reasons whatsoever," is "ineligible to retain a class ring." And: "Miniatures purchased through the contract manufacturer may be returned at the contract agreed price."

COLOR COMPANY

During the academic year, each Company and its members receive points for many aspects of Academy life—academics, athletics, and military performance. The Company garnering the most points becomes the Color Company for the next academic year, when the winning Company's members receive consequent privileges such as (for Firsties) parking their cars on The Yard in special areas. At the Color Parade during Commissioning Week, when the results of the year's competition are announced, a friend or the fiancée of the winning Company's Company Commander—designated Color Girl—transfers the flag from the old Color Company to the new. As yet, no commander of a Color Company has been a woman. When that happens, she will designate whomever she desires to join her in the transfer of colors.

COMMANDS

The Academy is one of about a dozen Annapolis area Navy and Marine commands. The one most closely tied to the Academy is the Naval Station, Annapolis—a subordinate command of the Academy's Superintendent. The role of the Naval Station is to support the Academy in various ways—to provide it with services, material, and enlisted personnel. Among its principal functions: to maintain the powered and sailing craft used to train midshipmen. Located across the Severn River from the Academy, the Naval Station has a Navy Exchange, a Commissary, and other services for Navy and Marine personnel; the Academy golf course is located there, as are shooting ranges for midshipman training and the 500-foot radio towers at Greenbury Point. The Naval Station also houses the Marines who perform guard duty at the Academy, including at the gates to The Yard and at the Chapel crypt of John Paul Jones.

COMMISSIONING WEEK

The culmination of four years by the Bay. If you're a parent or if you're otherwise lucky enough to be invited, go.

It begins in late May with the Dedication Parade, followed later that day by the Plebe Recognition Ceremony called Herndon [see below]. The week ends several days later with the hat toss following the awarding of diplomas and commissions (on the gridiron of Navy–Marine Corps Memorial Stadium, weather permitting). Mothers and/or drags traditionally pin ensign or second lieutenant boards on the shoulders of the new graduates; new graduates traditionally give a silver dollar to the first person who salutes them.

The intervening days are filled with festivities: parties, parades, dances (including the Ring Dance, when Second Class may begin wearing their class rings, and the Farewell Ball dating from 1865), receptions, and special events (capped by practice and formal performances by the Blue Angels, the Navy's aerial demonstration team).

Information about Commissioning Week doesn't arrive until late in the game—well into First Class year. Prudent parents of prospective graduates will make arrangements early (even several years early) for Commissioning Week accommodations—often an

Annapolis-area house. Generally, by September's First Class Parents Weekend (at the latest), parents sign up for a Commissioning Week house for the following May. Word of mouth is useful, but area housing and rental agencies are ordinarily the most helpful. Midshipmen in whatever class, or their parents, may make appointments with various owners to see their houses.

Aside from the frequently stifling heat, just about the only downside of Commissioning Week is the traffic; it can be gridlock (and be exacerbated by a Memorial Day Weekend parade and Blue Angels demonstrations). But the week is a major moment. Be there. And plan for it well in advance.

Oh, yes: And gifts are in order.

DATING

In the words of the catalogue, "Social life during Plebe year is limited." Well said. Officially, unless on leave, Plebes may date only with authorization from the Commandant, which occurs on about four weekends a year—plus during Commissioning Week. Plebes are discouraged from dating at other times; they are especially discouraged from seeing steadies during Plebe Summer. They may not escort dates on The Yard and, when in uniform, do so riskily outside The Yard.

During the academic year dating among Plebes is forbidden, as is dating between Plebes and upperclassmen. Dating among upperclassmen is acceptable, except when it occurs between two members of the same Company—that is, in the same chain of command. Perhaps 10 to 15 percent of upperclass midshipmen date within the Brigade.

Dating between midshipmen and civilians happens regularly, although opportunities to meet datable individuals are substantially fewer than for those attending civilian colleges. Upperclassmen often travel to places inhabited by the opposite sex; similarly, dates often travel to the Academy—particularly from the countless colleges and universities within a 100-mile radius of the Academy.

Public displays of affection (PDA) by midshipmen in uniform, on or outside The Yard, are not acceptable—just as they are not acceptable in the fleet.

THE DAY (OR THE ROUTINE)

5:30 A.M.—arise for personal fitness workout (optional)

6:30 A.M.—reveille (everyone is supposed to be out of bed)

7:00 A.M.—morning quarters formation

7:10 A.M.—breakfast

7:55 A.M.—first period begins

8:55 A.M.—second period begins

9:55 A.M.—third period begins

10:55 A.M.—fourth period begins

12:05 P.M.—noon meal formation (Note: Saturday's noon meal formation is at 10:15 A.M. to accommodate early liberty calls; upperclassmen have no Sunday noon meal formation, though Plebes have a Sunday formation at 1:00 P.M.)

12:15 P.M.—lunch

1:30 P.M.—fifth period begins

2:30 P.M.—sixth period begins

3:30 P.M.—seventh period begins (rarely used)

5:00 to 7:00 P.M.—buffet dinner

7:30 to 11:00 P.M.—study

10:00 P.M.—all upperclassmen must be on The Yard

11:00 P.M.—taps for Plebes (must be in Company areas) and lights out

Midnight—taps for upperclassmen (must be in Company areas)

(Note: Some midshipman schedules include eighth, ninth, and tenth periods; they are combined, or extended, morning periods for scheduling purposes.)

Regarding weekends: (1) there are no academic classes; (2) on Saturday nights, taps for all midshipmen is 1:00 A.M. Sunday; (3) taps on Sundays is identical to weekdays.

DRUGS AND ALCOHOL

Drugs are a zero-tolerance no-no. They're also illegal. In accordance with Navy-wide regulations and practices, midshipmen are subject to random urinalysis for the detection of drug use—with expulsion the certain consequence.

Regarding alcohol, the Academy adheres to Maryland's drinking age of 21. The Academy also encourages responsible use and severely punishes midshipmen in cases of abuse or misuse. In nearly all cases, Plebes (even those 21) may not drink except when away from the Academy on leave. Upperclassmen may drink in appropriate places if they are 21. Except when and where authorized by the Commandant, drinking is not permitted anywhere on The Yard (aside from in the Officers' Club). It almost never is permitted in Bancroft.

EXTRACURRICULARS

The Academy has about 100—from publications to academic and athletic clubs, from musical/theatrical groups to military and professional societies, from recreational and religious organizations to social-service ones. They are funded largely by the Midshipmen Welfare Fund, which annually receives nearly $1 million from Naval Academy Store profits.

To participate, midshipmen must have a 2.15 average. All ECAs except honor societies must have at least 20 members. And there's a category within the category: Certain activities, such as the Drum and Bugle Corps and the cheerleaders, are designated "Brigade support activities," which are exempt from drill and intramural sports requirements (ECAs are not). Generally, ECAs may meet only on Saturdays and from 7:15 to 8:00 on Sunday and Monday nights.

Names among the many include the Masqueraders, the Men's and Women's Glee Clubs, and the various choirs; nearly a dozen honor societies; the Scuba Club and the Airborne Training Unit; the Small Arms Club and Ultimate Frisbee; the Flying Club and the Yard Patrol Squadron; the *Lucky Bag* (yearbook) and *The Log* (humor magazine); the Black Studies Club and the Forensic Society; the Fellowship of Christian Athletes and the Jewish Midshipmen Club; Big Brothers/Big Sisters and the Midshipman Action Group; the Amateur Radio Club and WRNV. Each ECA has an officer representative and is carefully supervised.

FACILITIES

For anyone visiting The Yard, these are the hours that certain facilities are generally open to the public:

The Yard: 9:00 A.M. to 7:00 P.M. (or to sunset, whichever is later)

Chapel: 9:00 A.M. to 4:30 P.M. Monday–Saturday; 12:30 P.M. to 4:30 P.M. Sunday

Crypt: 9:00 A.M. to 4:30 P.M. Monday–Saturday; 12:15 P.M. to 4:30 P.M. Sunday

Museum: 9:00 A.M. to 5:00 P.M. Monday–Saturday; 11:00 A.M. to 5:00 P.M. Sunday

Library (when visitor is accompanied by a midshipman): 7:45 A.M. to 11:45 P.M. Monday–Friday; 7:30 A.M. to noon Saturday; 1:00 P.M. to 11:45 P.M. Sunday

Memorial Hall: 9:00 A.M. to 5:00 P.M. daily

Visitor Center: 9:00 A.M. to 5:00 P.M. daily; December–February, 9:00 A.M. to 4:00 P.M. daily

FOOTBALL

Several points:

(1) Arrive at the stadium well in advance of the game—in time to see both the march-over and the march-on. Those arriving after the march-over, for which traffic is halted, may encounter the mother of all traffic jams.

(2) Midshipmen are not permitted to be out of ranks prior to the game; nor are they allowed to leave the stadium prior to the game's end, including during halftime.

(3) Except for Firsties, midshipmen are not allowed to sit with parents and friends in the stands. Often the best way to see a particular midshipman during the game is to arrange ahead of time to meet at an agreed place in the stadium during halftime.

(4) Both NCAA and Academy rules prohibit alcohol sales in the stadium. Possession of alcohol in the stands is not allowed either; officials check for possession at the entrance gates.

(5) In the interest of building spirit, upperclass midshipmen often "bet" with Plebes on the outcome of football games for inoffensive, non-monetary stakes. Plebes, of course, pick Navy.

(6) All midshipmen attend all home games unless they (a) have duty, or (b) are away from the Academy.

See *Army-Navy Game* [above] and *Tailgating* and *Tickets* [below].

THE FOUNDATION

Actually, it's the U.S. Naval Academy Foundation, Inc. When formed in 1944 it was called the Alumni Foundation, but since has separated. It is distinct from the Alumni Association.

The Foundation enhances the academics of civilians (for the most part not particularly strong athletes) seeking Academy appointments. It raises money through contributions and membership dues.

The system works this way.

The Academy's Admissions Board automatically sends to the Foundation the applications of particularly promising candidates narrowly failing to get past the board for academic reasons. The Foundation contacts those it feels could gain admission with an additional year of school.

Willing Academy prospects apply to various prep schools, junior colleges, and colleges that work with the Foundation. If a given school accepts a given applicant for what is in effect a postgraduate year, the Foundation then sends the school an amount up to one-third of its fees—depending on the capacity of the prospect's family to pay them.

If the prospects perform well during the academic year (generally getting no Ds or Fs), and about 90 percent do, then the Academy practically assures them admission. Foundation applicants to the Academy must secure a nomination, even if they had one a year earlier. But the Foundation may actively assist in the gaining of an appointment.

The Academy enrolls about 100 through the Foundation program each year.

GIVING

The Academy has a number of entities that will gladly accept tax-deductible contributions. Among them:

—The Alumni Association (410-263-4448)
—The Athletic Association (800-US4-NAVY)
—The Foundation (410-267-8651)
—The Memorial Fund (410-263-4448 or 410-293-1546)
—The Museum Fund and General Gift Fund (410-293-1546)

—The Sailing Foundation (410-268-4894)
—The United States Naval Institute (410-268-6110)
The best way to obtain information on fund-raising is to contact the executive director of the Alumni Association.

HERNDON

The Academy calls it the Plebe Recognition Ceremony, but that's a losing effort. It's Herndon. And any parent or friend of a Plebe ought to see it.

What happens is this.

In late May, early in Commissioning Week, the Plebe Class rushes from T-Court in front of Bancroft to the Herndon Monument near the front of the Chapel.

Upperclassmen have greased the 21-foot granite obelisk with lard, crankcase grease, and whatever else they can imagine. At the top they have fixed—even fused—a dixie-cup sailor's hat.

Only when one of the Plebes replaces the dixie cup with a mid-shipman's cover do Plebes shuck the word and become officially members of the Fourth Class.

The distinction lasts but a short time—until Commissioning of the Firsties. No sooner do the (now former) Firsties toss their covers into the air than the (former) Fourth Classmen slap on their Youngster boards. Yet even then it is questionable whether they are truly Youngsters: Tradition has it that Fourth Classmen do not become Third Classmen—or Youngsters—until they see the dome of the Chapel upon returning from their Youngster cruise.

The Herndon Monument was erected in 1859 in memory of Commander William Herndon, who went down two years earlier with the mail steamer *Central America* in a storm off Cape Hatteras.

Some time before 1900 Plebes began celebrating the end of Fourth Class year by rushing from Dahlgren to Herndon. They began climbing the monument in about 1957. The first recorded time occurred in 1962, when the class of 1965 accomplished the task in three minutes.

The fastest time so far: 1 minute 30 seconds (class of 1972, in 1969).

The slowest time so far: 4 hours 15 minutes and 17 seconds (class of 1998, in 1995).

I-DAY....

...Or Induction Day.

Go, for sure.

Unless you live near Annapolis and can drive over that morning, get there the night before with your son or daughter, stay in an Annapolis hotel or motel, and celebrate. It will be his or her last chance to do that for a while.

And be on time the following morning.

The day will be as much a milestone in your life as it will be in his or hers.

After he or she disappears into Alumni Hall (and then is bused to Bancroft), you'll spend the rest of the day waiting for the Induction ceremony in T-Court at about 6 P.M. You can do a variety of things. Perhaps the best is to roam The Yard and get a feel for the place (in the process you just may catch a glimpse of your son or daughter). Top Academy officials hold a briefing for parents shortly after lunch. And Dahlgren Hall has numerous television sets showing videos and live coverage of I-Day processing.

The weather will almost certainly be broiler hot. Take a lot of film and/or videotape, a lot of Kleenex, maybe some reading, and a cooler. And get to T-Court well in advance of the Induction ceremony's appointed hour.

The procedure following the ceremony is for parents to gather on Stribling Walk at the letter corresponding to the first letter of their last name (or at some other agreed letter), to which the new midshipman will come at Induction's end.

You'll have about 15 minutes together. That's all.

MAIL

See *Address* [above].

MEDICAL AND DENTAL

As members of the federal armed forces, midshipmen receive all their medical and dental care free of charge.

The main medical clinic is on Hospital Point near Gate 8; bus service is provided from various points on The Yard throughout every day. Sick Call is several times daily for diagnosis and treatment. The medical staff and numerous visiting specialists also see midshipmen for routine check-ups, annual physicals, physical therapy, screenings, immunizations, orthopedics, and acute care. A duty crew remains available 24 hours a day.

Emergency patients are taken to Anne Arundel General Hospital and Medical Center in Annapolis, or to Baltimore—depending on the level of emergency care required. Serious long-term cases are treated within the Navy's hospital system, usually at the Bethesda Naval Medical Center near Washington, D.C.

Many parents retain their own health-insurance coverage on their midshipmen, on the grounds that unforeseen medical discharges from the Academy may render medical insurance after discharge—because of pre-existing condition—impossible to find.

Dental, in the basement of Bancroft's sixth wing, gives annual exams, cleanings, and fluoride treatments. It also provides just about all aspects of dental medicine, including oral surgery and limited orthodontics. Its staff sees patients either at morning and afternoon Sick Call Monday through Friday, or by appointment.

MILITARY TIME

The fundamental difference is that it's based on a 24-hour clock instead of a 12-hour one.

For A.M. times: 1:00 A.M. to 12:00 noon translates into 0100 hours to 1200 hours.

Simple.

Then, for P.M. times, add 12 and start over: 1:00 P.M. to 12:00 midnight translates into 1300 hours to 2400 hours.

Examples:

—1:30 A.M. is 0130
—1:15 P.M. is 1315
—8:40 P.M. is 2040

MOVING

The Navy or Marine Corps pays many of the moving expenses of all officers, including newly commissioned ensigns and second lieutenants.

A midshipman/officer arranges such a permanent change-of-duty move through the Academy's Personnel Property Division in Halligan Hall. That supply department division then contracts with an independent company for the move.

For payment purposes, the move may be from either the Academy or from one's home of record (usually a hometown) to one's new duty station.

THE MUSEUM

It's in Preble Hall and is open seven days a week. It has numerous displays and about 50,000 items.

The museum also plays a major role elsewhere on The Yard: notably John Paul Jones's crypt, Memorial Hall, and the various monuments—regarding all of which it acts variously as caretaker, curator of exhibits, and maintainer of property records and inventories.

See *Facilities* [above].

NAPS

The formal name is the Naval Academy Preparatory School (NAPS) in Newport, Rhode Island.

It began in Newport in 1915 with 13 enlisted sailors. It then moved to Norfolk, Virginia (1920), to the Bainbridge Naval Training Center about 40 miles north of Baltimore (1943), back to Newport (1950), back to Bainbridge (1951), and back to Newport (1975)—where it remains.

No one applies directly to NAPS. The Academy refers to NAPS those applicants it feels could profit from a year there prior to Academy admission. NAPS annually enrolls about 230; the Academy subsequently enrolls about 180 NAPSters.

NAPS's primary purpose is to strengthen the academics of Academy prospects from the fleet (including the Marines) and from the Naval Reserve—plus the academics of civilian minorities and athletes seeking Academy appointments. To attend NAPS, civilians must enlist in the Naval Reserve.

There is no fee—and no boot camp.

In August NAPSters begin a 10-month program of academics and military training. To win appointments to the Academy they must complete the Academy-oriented academics successfully (generally with a C average, no Fs, and no more than two Ds) and receive a favorable recommendation from the NAPS director.

. Those NAPSters gaining appointments do not need separate nominations to enter the Academy; they are sworn in on I-Day with other appointees, though they begin their processing a day earlier than non-NAPSters. Those failing or disenrolling from NAPS during the year may (a) return to the fleet to fulfill their fleet obligation, or (b) if they went to NAPS as civilians, return to civilian status.

THE NAVAL ACADEMY STORE

Located in the basement of Bancroft's first and third wings, the Naval Academy Store, formerly called (and still frequently called by midshipmen) the Mid Store, dates from 1867. It is the primary place where midshipmen do their shopping. It has more than 20,000 items—from snacks to engagement rings, from books to stereos, from T-shirts and tennis shoes to soap and socks.

In addition, the store has the largest selection of, and the best prices on, Navy/USNA-imprinted clothing and gifts anywhere. It also offers such services as monogramming, engraving, film developing, photocopying, and telegraph florist delivery.

The store is open to midshipmen in uniform, Academy faculty and staff, and active-duty military in uniform—as well as to anyone accompanied by them. Academy alumni are authorized to shop in the store on the weekends of all home football games.

Hours:

Monday–Friday 7:30 A.M. to 3:30 P.M.

Saturday 7:30 A.M. to noon

(Note: The store has extended hours for such events as Commissioning Week, I-Day, Parents Weekends, and Homecoming; it is closed on Sunday, during certain vacation periods, and on Saturday in the summer.)

Phone: 410-293-2392/2393

Nearby are other stores and services for the exclusive use of midshipmen and Academy-related personnel—including the cobbler shop, tailor shop, barber/beauty shop, uniform shop, laundry drop-off, and travel agency.

Academy Store revenues (from more than $20 million in sales annually) help fund about 100 extracurricular activities and club sports for the midshipmen—to the tune of nearly $1 million per year. Proceeds from the Visitor Center also benefit midshipmen activities.

THE NAVAL INSTITUTE

Formed in 1873 and headquartered in Preble Hall, the private and nonprofit U.S. Naval Institute promotes knowledge of the Navy and Marines.

Its principal roles are as book publisher (serving as the Academy's university press) and as publisher of the monthly *Proceedings* magazine. It also maintains a bookstore, book service, and research library. The bookstore is open daily, Monday–Saturday 9:00 A.M. to 5:00 P.M., and Sunday 11:00 A.M. to 5:00 P.M. It is closed New Year's Day, Easter, Thanksgiving, and Christmas.

In addition, the Naval Institute's 85,000 members receive discounts on various books, publications, photographs, prints, etc. And they may participate in seminars the Institute arranges.

Address: Preble Hall, 118 Maryland Avenue
Annapolis, Maryland 21402-5035
Phone: 410-268-6110 or 800-233-8764

NEWSPAPERS, ETC.

Midshipmen may buy subscriptions for delivery to their rooms by Plebes. Among the most popular and most readily available:

—The (Annapolis) *Capital*
—The *Baltimore Sun*
—The *New York Times*
—*USA Today*
—The *Wall Street Journal*
—The *Washington Post*
—The *Washington Times*

Midshipmen may also subscribe to magazines for delivery by mail.

Regarding radio: About three dozen AM and FM stations (including the midshipmen-run WRNV) based in Annapolis, Baltimore, and Washington, D.C., serve the Annapolis area. Upperclass midshipmen are allowed to have radios.

Regarding television: A number of network stations serve the Annapolis area from Baltimore, Washington, D.C., and Annapolis itself. The Academy does have access to some cable stations, accessible by Company wardroom TVs. Midshipmen may not have televisions in their rooms.

THE OFFICERS' CLUB

Actually, its formal name is the Officers' & Faculty Club. Sometimes it is called the O&F Club. More often it's the Officers' Club, or the O Club.

It is on The Yard near Gate 3. It has more than 3,200 dues-paying members.

Firsties wishing to become dues-paying members are assessed about $30 annually. They may use the O Club during periods of Yard, town, and weekend liberty and leave.

Second Classmen, Youngsters, and Plebes may not be members of the O Club, but may use certain of its facilities when on authorized liberty.

Plebes on liberty may use the facilities only when accompanied by their sponsor or by an immediate family member who is a member or is a guest of an active or retired military officer.

The O Club extends guest privileges to parents of midshipmen at any time—whether accompanied by their midshipman or not. And even if their midshipman has been commissioned, parents may use the O Club as unescorted visitors.

The club has several upstairs dining rooms, an upstairs bar, and a downstairs cocktail lounge.

Generally, the club serves (a) lunch Tuesday through Friday, (b) dinner Tuesday through Saturday, and (c) Sunday brunch. It has a happy hour Friday evenings with complimentary hors d'oeuvres. It is closed Mondays.

In addition, the club offers facilities for banquets, meetings, and special functions.

Phone: 410-263-8280.

OTHER ACADEMIES

There are four—all of which, like the Naval Academy, award Bachelor of Science degrees:

(1) *West Point,* also known as the *United States Military Academy* (USMA), on the Hudson River about 50 miles north of New York City, in Highland Falls, New York. Founded in 1802. Those attending are called cadets. Enrollment: by law, an authorized complement identical to the Naval Academy's. Class designations: Plebe, Yearling, Cow, Firstie. Graduates are commissioned as second lieutenants in the Army.

(2) *United States Air Force Academy,* in Colorado Springs, Colorado. Founded in 1954. Those attending are called cadets. Enrollment: by law, an authorized complement identical to the Naval Academy's. Class designations: Doolie, 3 Degree, 2 Degree, First Class. Graduates are commissioned as second lieutenants in the Air Force.

(3) *U.S. Coast Guard Academy,* on the Thames River in New London, Connecticut. Founded in 1876. Those attending are called cadets. Class designations: Fourth Class (Swabs during Fourth Class summer), Third Class, Second Class, and First Class. Enrollment: about 900. Graduates are commissioned as ensigns in the Coast Guard.

(4) *U.S. Merchant Marine Academy,* on Long Island in King's Point, New York. Founded in 1938. Those attending are called midshipmen. Class designations: Fourth Class (Plebes), Third Class, Second Class, First Class. Enrollment: about 1,000. Graduates may apply for active duty in any of the services. About 90 percent go into the Naval or Merchant Marine Reserve; the remainder go into other military branches.

PARADES

They are impressive. And nearly all midshipmen spend a good deal of time drilling for them.

Those who see home football games should remember that the march-over from the Academy to the football stadium is not a parade but a rather relaxed something-else.

Parades take place on the Worden Field parade ground. They are held on special occasions and periodically throughout the year—in late September and October (sometimes running into early November)—and in April. A few Plebe parades occur during the summer.

In addition, several parades are held during Commissioning Week—including the Dedication Parade and the Color Parade (the last parade in which Firsties march as midshipmen).

PARENTS WEEKENDS
There are two.

One is Plebe Parents Weekend. Probably the most important event for parents during their midshipman's entire four years, it occurs in mid-August at the end of Plebe Summer. In most cases it will provide the first opportunity to see your new midshipman since I-Day—and for him or her to see you. Be there. Get a hotel or motel room. Stay for the duration. Do whatever your Plebe wants to do. And remain positive, supportive, and upbeat.

The other is Firstie Parents Weekend. It usually occurs in early September. Perhaps less important than Plebe Parents Weekend, it nevertheless provides an opportunity to see your son or daughter in the Academy environment as he or she begins the last Academy year.

A final note: Under normal circumstances, these are the only two routine opportunities to see a midshipman's room. Yet the Command Duty Officer may authorize a parent or guardian to visit a midshipman's room on occasions that are not formal Parents Weekends.

PARKING
It's tight on The Yard; the police enforce parking regulations vigorously. And remember that the Naval Academy is a federal facility: Parking violations (as well as moving violations, especially speeding) find resolution in a federal magistrate system.

That goes for midshipmen as well—and for Academy graduates in training or on duty at Navy or Marine facilities around the country; an efficient computer system relentlessly tracks down miscreants.

Parking violations carry stiff fines. When visiting The Yard, park only in lots or where the surface or curbs are unpainted. Do not park where curbs are painted white (government and/or military vehicles only), yellow (officers only), or red (police and fire only). And do not park in front of the quarters on Porter, Upshur, and Rodgers Roads marked with resident parking signs.

In Annapolis, parking is available in six public-access facilities. On-street parking, in both metered and non-metered areas, is limited to two hours and is generally nearly impossible to find. Parking is always available at Navy–Marine Corps Stadium, with shuttle service to the Academy and downtown.

PICTURES AND VIDEOS

In the fall of every year, the studio that has won the contract for photographs of midshipmen visits the Academy. It takes pictures of all midshipmen, in uniform: Classes alternate between full dress blues (FDBs) and choker whites; Firsties must have their yearbook pictures taken in FDBs; First Class athletes may also have a picture taken in their letter sweater. Proofs go separately to parents and midshipmen in time for selections to be made and prints received by Christmas.

Parents periodically receive mailings from contracting studios about videos: of Plebe Summer, of each academic year, of Herndon, of Commissioning Week, etc.; some of the videos offer the option of including footage of one's son or daughter in the video—an option, if selected, with which the midshipman would need to cooperate.

PUBLICATIONS

Those run by midshipmen are

—*The Lucky Bag* (yearbook)
—*Reef Points* (an annual for Plebes)
—*The Labyrinth* (the annual literary magazine)

In addition, there are these publications:

—*The Trident* (a weekly tabloid newspaper published by the Academy's Public Affairs Office—phone: 410-293-5355).

—*Shipmate* (a monthly alumni magazine published by the Alumni Association).

—*Naval History* (a quarterly published by the Naval Institute).

—*Proceedings* (a monthly magazine on Navy and Marine matters, with articles from time to time about the Academy, published by the Naval Institute).

—*Articles Adrift* (an occasional publication of the USNA Parents and Sponsors Club of Maryland; address available through the Alumni Association).

—*All Hands,* published by the Navy.

—*Navy Times.*

Finally, the Academy's Public Affairs Office can suggest a number of ways—published and electronic—for learning more about Yard events and activities affecting midshipmen (see *Telephones* [below]).

SPONSORS

During Plebe Summer, under what is dubbed the Plebe Sponsor Program, every new midshipman who desires is linked with a family inside a 22-mile radius of the Academy; when a family knows an incoming midshipman, the link can be easily prearranged.

Such volunteer families, or sponsors, serve as homes away from home—not only for Plebes but for midshipmen during their entire Academy careers. Sponsors frequently become key connections with the world beyond the wall—as well as friends for life.

SYNAGOGUE

See *Worship* [below].

TAILGATING

It's a long tradition at football games, and a growing one at other athletic events such as crew and lacrosse.

At home football games, the entire parking area surrounding the stadium is available for tailgating. Spreads range from the bare minimum to the far-out elaborate.

A guideline: If midshipmen will be dropping by a tailgate following the game (they are not available prior to the game and at halftime), be sure to (a) have what they like, yet (b) abide by Academy rules and Maryland laws relating to alcohol.

Regarding tailgating at non-football events: Go with the flow.

See *Football* [above] and *Tickets* [below].

TAKE-OUT

Some Annapolis eateries deliver to midshipmen at the Academy. But there's a hitch. Drivers of telephoned orders for, say, pizza and Chinese foods are directed to either Gate 1 or Gate 3. There midshipmen pay the drivers for the order and return to Bancroft—or wherever.

Some local bakeries and florists will also deliver gifts or prepaid items for midshipmen to Bancroft's Main Office.

TELEPHONES

For the most part, midshipmen don't write. They call. Midshipmen may not have telephones (except cellular) in their rooms, but Bancroft has numerous banks of pay phones. A prudent arrangement for parents is to have their midshipman call at a regular time each week.

Because most midshipmen do not have their own telephone numbers, telephone charge cards tied to such telephone numbers are impossible for midshipmen to obtain. But they may acquire non-subscriber charge cards or military calling cards through the telephone company. The cards permit the charging of long-distance calls anywhere in the country, but certain cards require payment of bills within several weeks (the phone company blocks all additional charges to delinquent accounts).

Calls to midshipmen are best made through the Main Office (410-293-5001/5002/5003). Telephones there are manned 24 hours a day. A message for a specific midshipman will usually be delivered to his or her room within minutes; many are sent by electronic mail. If the caller knows the midshipman's room number, or at least the class and Company, sometimes that information enhances the already high likelihood of the message making it to the right room. Rather than leaving lengthy messages, in most cases the caller simply should ask the midshipman to call (immediately or at his or her convenience) a specific number or individual.

In major emergencies, when calling the Main Office does not seem to be eliciting a swift enough response by a midshipman, a call to his or her Battalion Office may speed things along.

Key Academy telephone numbers:

AREA CODE: 410
Main Operator (and Information).....293-1000
Main Office (Bancroft).....293-5001/5002/5003
Battalion Offices (Messages):
    First (Companies 1–6).....293-7100
    Second (Companies 7–12).....293-7200
    Third (Companies 13–18).....293-7300
    Fourth (Companies 19–24).....293-7400
    Fifth (Companies 25–30).....293-7500
    Sixth (Companies 31–36).....293-7600
Action-Information Line (Public Affairs).....293-3109
Admissions Office.....293-4361
Alumni Association.....263-4448
Athletic Association.....800-US4-NAVY
    Tickets.....268-6060
Athletic Director.....293-2429
Candidate Guidance.....293-4361/4844
Chamber of Commerce (Annapolis).....268-7676
Chaplain's Office.....293-1100
Commandant's Office.....293-7005
Dean's Office.....293-1583
Directory Assistance.....293-1000
Division of Engineering and Weapons.....293-6310/6311
Division of Humanities and
    Social Sciences.....293-6300/6301
Division of Mathematics and Science.....293-6330/6332
Division of Professional Development.....293-6000/6001
Gift Shop.....268-3355
Midshipmen Activities Officer.....293-7135
Midshipmen Legal Adviser.....293-2268/4188
Museum.....293-2108
Musical Activities.....293-2439

Naval Academy Store.....293-2392/2393
Naval Institute.....268-6110
Naval Station and Navy Exchange.....757-0005
NFCU.....268-0043
Officers' Club.....263-8280
Public Affairs.....293-2291/2292/2293
Sponsor Program.....293-7128
Sports News.....800-US4-NAVY, 267-NAVY/2340, 268-6226
Superintendent's Office.....293-1500
Trident Newspaper.....293-5355
Visitor Center
    Tours.....263-6933
    Gift Shop.....268-3355

TICKETS

The Naval Academy Athletic Association sells all tickets to Navy football games; such tickets are available individually or for the full home-game season. A low-cost membership in the NAAA provides certain benefits, including savings on season tickets. Season tickets generally offer better location and per-ticket discounts. The NAAA also sells tickets to other spectator sports, notably basketball.

The NAAA is located in Ricketts Hall.

Phone: 293-4955, 268-6060, or 800-US4-NAVY.

See *Football* and *Tailgating* [above].

Sponsors of various non-athletic events usually organize ticket sales—either independently or through the NAAA Ricketts' ticket office (notably those held in Alumni Hall such as the Masqueraders' fall drama and the Glee Club's winter musical). Tickets are not ordinarily necessary for the talent show in early spring.

Band concerts, lectures (including Forrestal lectures), and parades are usually free, open to the public, and require no tickets. Some concerts by well-known performers are held at the Academy principally for midshipmen, but tickets may be available to the public— through the NAAA ticket office—two weeks prior to the event.

TOBACCO

Its use is discouraged and, in most places, forbidden. Midshipmen may, however, smoke in their rooms if everyone in the room is a smoker (but they may not smoke in bed); otherwise, they may smoke in designated areas. Some smoke; some chew tobacco.

TOURS

Guided walking tours of the Academy are handled by the Guide Service operated out of the Armel-Leftwich Visitor Center; the service gives about 100,000 tours a year.

The hours for the Visitor Center are, *every day* except Thanksgiving, Christmas, and New Year's Day,

> March–November.....9:00 A.M. to 5:00 P.M.
> December–February.....9:00 A.M. to 4:00 P.M.

The hours for walking tours are

> December–February
>   Monday–Saturday.....11:00 A.M. and 1:00 P.M.
>   Sunday.....12:30 P.M. and 2:30 P.M.
> March–Memorial Day
>   Monday–Friday.....10:00 A.M. to 3:00 P.M. on the hour
>   Saturday.....10:00 A.M. to 3:30 P.M. on the half-hour
>   Sunday.....12:30 P.M. to 3:30 P.M. on the half-hour
> June–Labor Day
>   Monday–Saturday.....9:30 A.M. to 3:30 P.M. on the half-hour
>   Sunday.....12:30 P.M. to 3:30 P.M. on the half-hour
> September–November
>   Monday–Friday.....10:00 A.M. to 3:00 P.M. on the hour
>   Saturday.....10:00 A.M. to 3:30 P.M. on the half-hour
>   Sunday.....12:30 P.M. to 3:30 P.M. on the half-hour

(Note: During the academic year [except December–February], on Monday through Friday the noon tour departs the Visitor Center at 11:45 A.M. to enable visitors to see noon meal formation.)

Phone: Visitor Center (tours).....410-263-6933
              Fax.....410-263-7682
              Gift Shop.....410-268-3355

In addition, about half a dozen commercial guide companies based in Annapolis give tours of the Annapolis historic area, the State House area, and the waterfront; some give tours of the Academy as well. Their telephone numbers are widely available, or call the Annapolis Visitors Center at 410-280-0445. Anyone taking a tour by pedicab (available downtown) should be advised that the Academy does not permit pedicabs on The Yard.

See *Annapolis* and *Boat Shows* [above].

THE TOWN

See *Annapolis* [above].

TRANSPORTATION

When in Annapolis, the options for going elsewhere without one's own car are these:

—Cabs.
—Car rentals.
—Shuttle buses.
—A commuter bus to the New Carrollton Metro, which one may then board for Washington. D.C. (The Metro is easy and inexpensive for getting around the city.)
—Limousines from various points in Annapolis to Baltimore-Washington International Airport (BWI).

When not in Annapolis, the options for getting there without a car are these:

—Buses from Washington, D.C., and Baltimore.
—Cabs.
—Airport limousines and shuttle vans from Baltimore-Washington International (BWI) to Annapolis. Cabs from Washington National and Dulles airports to Annapolis.

Limousines from National and Dulles to BWI and the New Carrollton Metro.

Upperclass midshipmen may rent cars if they meet a given company's stipulated age for rental. Such ages vary from company to company.

Numbers:

Baltimore-Washington International Airport: 410-859-7111, 800-435-9294
Dulles International Airport: 703-661-2700
Washington National Airport: 800-421-7574

MARC: 800-325-RAIL
AMTRAK: 800-USA-RAIL
Baltimore Metro: 410-539-5000
Washington Metro: 202-637-7000

TRAVEL

As members of the military, midshipmen may receive considerable savings from commercial airlines and car-rental companies. Some airlines require that as a condition of such savings, midshipmen travel in uniform and show their green military ID on request. In general one-way military rates are quite inexpensive; yet regular round-trip non-refundable tickets may be less expensive than military fares.

A midshipman-oriented travel service—SATO—operates in the basement of Bancroft's fifth wing.

In addition, midshipmen may travel space-available on Military Airlift Command (MAC) flights between domestic and foreign military facilities. Washington's Andrews Air Force Base is the facility closest to the Academy for space-available opportunities.

Scheduling reliability on MAC flights is iffy, rendering their use questionable for midshipmen with strict travel deadlines.

VISITING

See *Parents Weekends* and *Tours* [above].

WEDDINGS

They happen, though they'd better not happen before graduation if a midshipman expects to remain at the Academy.

Chapel weddings are common—often back-to-back, every hour on the hour—immediately following Commissioning Week (as many as 30 may occur in that week). The schedule is determined by a raffle during the academic year. As many as 100 Chapel weddings occur at other times as well.

Arrangements should begin at least a year in advance. The Chaplain's Office (410-293-1100) offers pre-marriage counseling. It also has a handbook containing wedding information and an application for a Chapel ceremony.

Other important numbers:

Director of Musical Activities: 410-293-2439
Alumni Association: 410-263-4448
Officers' Club: 410-263-8280
Marriage License Information: 410-222-1434

WORSHIP

Attendance at worship services is encouraged but not required. Midshipmen may attend the Chapel for Catholic and Protestant services on Sunday, and the All Faiths Chapel in Mitscher Hall for Jewish services on Friday evenings.

In addition, Catholic masses and Protestant devotionals and communions are held variously in Mitscher and in St. Andrew's Chapel (in the main Chapel's lower level).

Midshipmen may also attend churches or synagogues in Annapolis.

And the Academy's seven chaplains offer counseling and denominational instruction.

The chaplains' telephone: 410-293-1100.

THE YEAR

Schedules for the year are commonplace at the Academy, but they do not often find their way to parents. If midshipmen do not provide them, a call to the Public Affairs Office should be able to elicit one.

These are the highlights:

Mid-August—summer leave ends; first semester begins
Labor Day—holiday
Columbus Day—holiday
Veterans' Day—holiday
Thanksgiving—leave: from last obligation on the Wednesday before Thanksgiving until leave expires on the Sunday following (four days)
Early December—Army-Navy game
Mid-December—exams begin (they last about a week; midshipmen may begin Christmas leave following their last exam; leave lasts two to three weeks)
Early January—Christmas leave ends; Intersessional (several days of general in-class military training); second semester begins
Martin Luther King Day (January)—holiday
Presidents' Day (February)—holiday
Early March—spring leave begins; lasts for about 10 days (one week and two weekends)
Early May—exams begin (they last about a week)
Mid-May—Intersessional (several days of general in-class military training), followed by Commissioning Week
Late May—Commissioning Week
Late May/Early June—summer leave and summer training begin
Late June/Early July—induction of the new Plebe class

FOR MORE INFORMATION

The Naval Academy appears in countless novels and nonfiction, either by reference or as a central setting, and in many movies.

Books

Among the best-known fiction are

—*Annapolis Ahoy!* (by Casper Blackburn, 1945)
—*Annapolis Misfit* (by Kurt Schmidt, 1974)
—*Annapolis Plebe* (by John H. Keatley, 1957)

—*Buck Jones at Annapolis* (by Richmond Hobson, 1907)
—*Dave Darrin's [Years] at Annapolis* (by Harrie Irving
  Hancock, 1911)
—*David Farragut, Boy Midshipman* (by Laura Long, 1950)
—*Fought for Annapolis* (by Fitzhugh Green, 1925)
—*Midshipman Lee of the Naval Academy* (by Robb White,
  1954)
—*Navy Blue and Gold, A Story of the Naval Academy*
  (by George Bruce, 1936)
—*Navy Blue: A Story of Cadet Life in the United States
  Naval Academy at Annapolis* (by Willis Boyd Allen, 1898)
—*Patriot Games* (by Tom Clancy, 1987)
—*The Return of Philo T. McGiffin* (by David Poyer, 1983)
—*A Sense of Honor* (by James Webb, 1981)

Among the voluminous nonfiction:

—*The Annapolis Story: Blue and Gold* (by Paul Ilyinsky, 1974)
—*Annapolis: The Life of a Midshipman, a Picture Story* (by
  Jack Engeman, 1956)
—*Annapolis Today* (by Kendall Banning, 1963)
—*One Hundred Years of the U.S. Naval Academy* (by Wells
  L. Field, 1946)
—*Brigade Seats!: The Naval Academy Cookbook* (by Karen
  Gibson, 1993)
—*Marine Officer's Guide* (by LCOL Kenneth W. Estes, USMC,
  1985)
—*The Naval Academy Candidate Book* (by William L. Small-
  wood, 1989)
—*Naval Officer's Guide* (by VADM William P. Mack, USN
  [Ret.], 1991)
—*A Place Called The Yard* (by Margaret H. Edsall, 1976,
  revised 1992)
—*Service Etiquette* (by Oretha D. Swartz, 1988)
—*The Story of the Naval Academy* (by Felix Riesenberg, 1958)
—*The United States Naval Academy, Being a Yarn of the
  American Midshipman* (by Park Benjamin, 1900)

—*United States Naval Academy, the First Hundred Years* (by John de Murinelly Cirne Crane, 1945)
—*The U.S. Naval Academy: an Illustrated History* (by Jack Sweetman, 1979; revised 1995)
—*U.S. Naval Academy: A Pictorial Celebration of 150 Years* (by Ellen B. Heinbach and Gale G. Kohlhagen, 1995)

Movies

A number of generally old movies have the Naval Academy as a central or peripheral theme. Some may appear on late-night TV or may be available on video (time lengths are given if possible). Among them:

—*Annapolis* (1928, starring John Mack Brown and Jeanette Loff)
—*Annapolis Farewell* (1935, 75 minutes, starring Robert Taylor)
—*Annapolis Salute* (1937, 65 minutes, starring Van Heflin, James Ellison, Arthur Lake, and Harry Carey)
—*An Annapolis Story* (1955, 81 minutes, color, starring John Derek, Kevin McCarthy, and Diana Lynn)
—*The Midshipman* (1925 [silent], starring Ramon Novarro, Harriet Hammond, and William Boyd)
—*Midshipman Jack* (1933, 73 minutes, starring Bruce Cabot and Betty Furness)
—*Minesweeper* (1943, 67 minutes, starring Richard Arlen and Jean Parker)
—*Naval Academy* (1941, 67 minutes, starring Freddie Bartholomew)
—*Navy Blue and Gold* (1937, 63 minutes, starring Jimmy Stewart, Robert Young, and Lionel Barrymore)
—*Patriot Games* (1992, 114 minutes, starring Harrison Ford, Anne Archer, James Earl Jones, and Thora Birch)
—*Pride of the Navy* (1939, 63 minutes, starring James Dunn)
—*Salute* (1929, starring George O'Brien, Helen Chandler, Stepin Fetchit, and John Wayne)
—*Saturday's Hero* (1951, starring John Derek, Aldo Ray, and Donna Reed)

—*Shipmates* (1931, 73 minutes, starring Robert Montgomery)
—*Shipmates Forever* (1935, 109 minutes, starring Dick
    Powell and Ruby Keeler)
—*The Splinter Fleet* (1939, starring Wallace Beery and Mar-
    jorie Main)

In addition, many movies deal with various aspects of Navy and
Marine history. And constantly released videos highlight just about
every aspect of the Navy and Marine Corps.

NAVAL ACADEMY AT ANNAPOLIS, MARYLAND. 1853

9 / GLOSSARY: DEFINITION, TERMS ACRONYMS, SLANG

Language at the Naval Academy *lives.* It is ever changing, yet ever the same.

The following is a compendium of defined terms, slang, abbreviations, and acronyms seen and heard in all the Academy's right (and not so right) places. It is offered as an aid to understanding the vernacular of The Yard and those who inhabit it.[*]

Academic Accountability—the requirement that midshipmen attend all their classes (and be on time) unless they have valid excuses. They are marked absent if they are late.

Academic Adviser—a teacher within a midshipman's major assigned to him or her for academic guidance and course selection.

Academic Board—a review board that convenes at the end of each semester to consider poor academic and military performance, and to determine which of those midshipmen qualifying for separation

[*] Note: Except in cases of certain proper names, words appearing in italics indicate a separate entry.

shall be retained on probation (midshipmen failing to maintain satisfactory academic progress are technically separated); its members are the Superintendent, the Commandant, the Dean, and the four division directors—with the Director of Admissions serving as secretary and the Director of Athletics offering advice as necessary; called by midshipmen an *Ac Board* or (more affectionately) an *Axe Board;* see *Advisory Board.*

Academic Log—in each Company area, a log for entries by midshipmen regarding their *academic accountability*—that is, X midshipman notes that he missed or was late for Y class for Z reason.

Academically Deficient—(also Academically Unsat); a midshipman with a CQPR below 2.0 is academically deficient and must undertake corrective study measures as outlined by his or her Company Officer; a midshipman with a CQPR below 2.15—or with two Ds or one F in a semester—is not *weekend eligible;* see *gravy.*

Academic Tracking Sheets—forms, or study logs, that all *unsat* midshipmen must fill out to show how they have spent their study hours; also known by midshipmen as "weekly honor violations."

Ac (pronounced *ack*) Board (or *Axe Board*)—see *Academic Board.*

Advisory Board—a board, lower than the *Academic Board,* that meets at the end of each semester with midshipmen regarding academic difficulties and decides such things as whether they will repeat a failed course, change a major, attend summer school, etc.

Aero—short for aeronautical engineering, or for a midshipman majoring in it.

Affirmative—a military-wide term for "yes"; see *negative.*

Airdale—a military-wide nickname for an aviator, used most frequently by sailors.

Air Force Academy—"The Bus Driver School," in Colorado Springs, Colorado; its class designations—in order—are: Doolie, 3 Degree, 2 Degree, Firstie; see *classes* and *West Point.*

Alcohol—the law is 21 in Maryland; on The Yard alcohol may be consumed legally and within Academy regulations only by of-age midshipmen when and where approved by the Commandant (usually, on stipulated occasions, in Dahlgren, the Sailing Center, Hubbard Hall, Alumni Hall, and at the O Club); the misuse of alcohol by midshipmen is a severely fry-able offense (see *fry*), and all such offenses are dealt with by the Commandant.

All-Calls—a requirement, as punishment, that a Plebe perform *chow calls* more frequently than usual—for instance, every minute for 10 minutes before breakfast and lunch, instead of just 10 minutes and 5 minutes before.

Alpha Code—an identifying six-digit number given to every midshipman on Induction Day, and used throughout one's Naval Academy career on everything from forms to gear; the first two digits indicate the year of graduation.

AMCMO—acronym for Assistant Midshipman in Charge of Main Office, a Youngster billet.

Amnesty—see *presidential pardon*.

Anchor—(1) the midshipman with the lowest *order of merit* in the class, also called the Anchorman (the Firstie who graduates last in the class receives a dollar from every classmate—and among those close, competition is often keen); the lowest-rated anything (individual or unit); (2) the central, or crossing, point of the *T* in King Hall—where prior to meals the *bell* is rung, announcements are given, the prayer is said, and determined declarations are made to beat the next beleaguered athletic opponent.

Another Great (or Fine) Navy Day—a sardonic Navy-wide phrase of pretended, or mock, exuberance.

Another Great Navy Deal—*not* a good deal.

Area Tour—see *tour.*

Army Week—the week preceding the Army game, featuring activities and pranks designed to promote Brigade spirit.

ARRUGAH!—a version of the Marine motivational call, or grunt; see *HOO-YAH!* and *OO-RAH!*

Article—a Plebe *rate;* generally, the requirement that a Plebe read two front-page articles and one sports-page article in the daily newspaper, and be able to converse at least three minutes about each.

ASAP—military-wide acronym for As Soon As Possible.

ASTB—abbreviation for Aviation Selection Test Battery, a 2.5-hour, 5-part test for prospective aviators; it has a math/verbal section similar to the SAT, as well as parts on mechanical comprehension, spatial perception, aviation and nautical information, and aviation interest; offered in Second Class year; those failing to meet the minimum requirements are ineligible for flight assignments.

Attrition Classes—those classes with traditionally high failure rates, which thereby raise the Academy's attrition rate—notably chemistry for Plebes, physics for Youngsters, and electrical engineering (*double-e*) for Second Class.

Augmentation—a Navy-wide term for moving from the reserve to the regular service; also a verb: to augment up.

Aweigh—as in anchor's aweigh: when the anchor is free of the bottom, meaning the ship can get under way.

AWOL—military-wide acronym for Absent Without Leave; see *UA*.

Axe Board (or *Ac Board*)—see *Academic Board*.

Backseater (or Backseat Driver)—nickname for a Naval Flight Officer; see *NFO*.

Bag It—(noun) a slacker or lazy person; (verb) to take the easy route in something difficult, to give considerably less than one's best effort ("Out there on the track, I'm going to bag it and hope for the best"); see *dog it*.

Bancroft—Bancroft Hall; home sweet home; routinely called *the Hall* and (now infrequently) *Mother B.*

Barn—one of a few large rooms in Bancroft containing four roommates (more or less); see *rooming*.

The Basic Responses—see *responses*.

The Basic School—in Quantico, Virginia: where Marine second lieutenants go for training after graduation; also called *TBS*.

Basket Leave—(1) 30 days of leave given to all Naval Academy midshipmen upon graduation, and to be used within 90 days; (2) any leave not counted against an officer's allotted 30 days of leave per year.

Batt-O—short for Battalion Office; overseen by the Battalion Officer of the Watch (*BOOW* or *Bow Wow*)—a Firstie—and where the *MCBO*—a Second Class—stands duty and oversees the *BOM*—a Plebe.

Battalion—a unit of organization within the Brigade, which has 6 Battalions (3 per Regiment) and 36 Companies.

Battalion Office—see *Batt-O.*

Battalion Officer (Batt Officer)—a commissioned officer (commander, captain, or Marine lieutenant colonel or colonel) in administrative charge of six Companies; above a Company Officer and below the Deputy Commandant; see *Batt-O.*

Beat Army!—THE cry; the CRY.

Beat Feet—(verb) to get out or leave in a big hurry ("Let's beat feet; let's go").

Bed Check—usually on weekends, an after-hours check to determine the presence of midshipmen in their rooms.

The Bell—(1) the electronic bell that rings for reveille and classes; (2) the bell at the central point (the *Anchor*) of King Hall; (3) the bell in *T-Court* rung at the conclusion of each sports season by each varsity athlete who contributed to a victory over Army.

Ben "Obi-Wan" Kenobi—from the movie *Star Wars:* the often-invoked authority on matters relating to midshipmen of the opposite sex, notably when a dating relationship between two seems to be blossoming; a non-involved midshipman might say to his or her roommate: "Don't give in to the dark side. Don't be tempted by *Lima Victor*"; see *Dark Side.*

Best Orders—one's last orders, or the next ones.

Bilge—(verb) (1) to undercut, stab in the back, make another look bad ("Don't bilge your classmate"); also used as a noun (that is: a bilge or bilger, one who bilges another), and sometimes expanded to the full phrase ("He's a real bilge pump"); (2) to fail a course or class, or to leave the Academy for academic reasons (i.e., to "bilge out").

Bill—the goat; the Academy mascot off and on since 1893, when a goat named El Cid appeared at an Army-Navy football game in which Navy prevailed, 6-4; in the subsequent decade a dog, two cats, and a carrier pigeon served briefly as mascots, but Bill has been the official thing since 1904; he is trotted out for football games and pep rallies; Bill is either of two mascot rams kept at the Academy's 860-acre dairy in Gambrills, Maryland; a bronze goat statue stands near Lejeune Hall just inside Gate 1.

Billet—a Navy-wide term for a position, job, designation, duty assignment, slot, or space ("He got a billet to go air," or "My Company billet is...," or "They ran out of billets").

Birth Control Glasses (BCGs)—see *geekers.*

Birthday Ball—a dance celebrating the November 10 birthday of the Marine Corps; attended by Marine officers, senior enlisted, and prior-enlisted Marines who are currently midshipmen—plus their wives (if they are married officers) or dates.

Black Monday (or Sunday)—(1) any day on which the Brigade returns from leave, notably the Monday following Christmas leave and beginning the *Dark Ages;* (2) the night of the day parents leave from Plebe Parents Weekend at the end of Plebe Summer, a time of particular anxiety for Plebes, who then await (within about a week, called *Reorganization Week*) the *return of the Brigade.*

Black N—an "I've been bad" letter sweater, worn for the distinction of having incurred within a certain period too many (1) demerits (generally 100 or more), and/or (2) fry-able offenses (generally one 6,000 fry at all, or two 5,000 fries in a semester).

Blackshoe—a Navy-wide nickname for a surface warfare officer; often called a "shoe."

Blocks—the three segments of summer training, called First, Second, and Third Blocks; each is about a month long; in the summers preceding Youngster and Second Class years, at least one block must be (for Youngsters) a YP cruise and (for Second Class) a surface or submarine (gray hull) cruise; in another block Youngsters and Second Class have various experiences [see chapter 4, "Summer Training"]; summer training for First Class consists of a cruise and/or training in their prospective warfare assignment following their final Christmas leave; all midshipmen also may take an elective in the summer if compatible with a block of leave; the designation of which blocks each midshipman will serve, and where, is made in the spring by the Division of Professional Development's Department of Professional Programs based largely on availability, the midshipman's stated preferences, and his or her class rank.

Blood Pins—any insignia awarded for military achievement, such as (at the Academy) airborne (blood wings) or scuba; the phrase comes from the rite of smacking such pins (e.g., aviation wings, the submariner "dolphin," the SEAL "Budweiser" or "bird," etc.), with their two prongs in back, into the wearer's chest—usually drawing blood.

Blow Off—(verb) to pay insufficient attention to, as in "He blew her off" or "Of course he flunked chem. He blew it off all year."

Blue and Gold—(1) short for "Navy Blue and Gold," the Academy alma mater [see appendix for text]; (2) the Academy's official colors; (3) short for Blue and Gold Officer, any of many Academy alumni and friends throughout the country who provide information to prospective midshipmen and assist them in the admissions process.

Blue Carpet—the Commandant's area of Bancroft, on 4-1 in the fourth wing off the Rotunda.

The Blue Jackets' Manual—since 1902, the basic handbook of information for sailors; a Navy primer.

Blue Magnet—a nickname for a *rack* (bed), taken from the color of the bedspread; often, the bedspread itself; formerly the "blue trampoline."

Blue Rim—the standard-issue midshipman T-shirt, the top half of PE-issue gear.

Board—(1) a hearing or any formal session with any of various boards, be it *Academic, Advisory, Conduct, Performance,* etc.; (2) short for *shoulder board.*

Boats—nickname for a required engineering/naval architecture course; advanced students and those majoring in the area take *ships.*

BOHICA—an acronym for a number of Academy phrases, one of which is "But Oh, How I Can Achieve."

Bogus—slang for (1) something inferior or fake, and (2) a bad or unfair deal ("She was fried for not knowing the name of the president of Finland? That's bogus.").

BOM (pronounced *bomb*)—acronym for Battalion Office Messenger, a Plebe or Youngster on duty in the *Batt-O* with the *BOOW* and the *MCBO.*

Bone—a bad deal ("He got the bone"); also a verb ("That prof boned us with that test").

Boom!—an exclamation widely used in midshipman conversation to convey a sudden occurrence, as in "So there I was, about to wing the snowball, and—boom!—there's the Dant! Needless to say, I dropped it and walked casually on my way."

Boondocker—a standard-issue low boot, higher than an oxford but not a full boot; issued to all midshipmen.

BOOW—acronym for Battalion Officer of the Watch—a Firstie; also called the "Bow Wow."

Bow Wow—see *BOOW.*

Brace Up—(verb) regarding Plebes: to assume an exaggerated position of attention while producing as many chins as possible: chin tucked into the neck cavity, eyes straight ahead; bracing—the noun form—is a required Plebe rite exhibiting motivation and submission; now prohibited in King Hall.

Brag Sheet—a paper prepared by a midshipman about himself or herself, setting down the midshipman's achievements for consideration in determining his or her performance rating; a Navy-wide term.

Brain-Dump—(verb) (1) to purge the mind, to empty it of every pertinent thing following the need to know it ("Now that the year is over, I'm brain-dumping chemistry"); (2) to unload everything in the mind regarding a subject—such as during a test ("When I saw the question, I knew I had studied the right thing, and I just brain-dumped").

Brassard—a band of cloth worn around the upper sleeve, indicating a temporary duty assignment (such as watch or usher).

Bravo Zulu—or BZ, from the standard code book and phonetic alphabet: a Navy-wide term meaning well done ("a BZ—or Bravo Zulu—performance"); from the letters on signal flags hoisted on ships of the line.

Brick—a brick that Plebes give their Company's upperclassman who had the weekend's most objectionable date; in single file, Plebes shuffle rhythmically through their Company area (chanting, "The brick. The brick. Who gets the brick?"); the line stops outside the winner's door and the leader awards the brick; illegal.

Brigade—the collective noun for all the midshipmen as a group: the Brigade of Midshipmen; see *Regiment, Battalion, Company, Platoon,* and *Squad.*

Brownshoe—a Navy-wide nickname for an aviation officer (pilot or *NFO*).

Brush Off—(verb) to remove the lint from one's uniform—frequently with a whisk broom or tape—as in one roommate saying to another, "Hey, quick: Brush (or tape) me off."

B.S.—(1) the degree (Bachelor of Science) granted to all graduating midshipmen, even *bull majors* (some say nothing could be better than to have a B.S. in, for instance, English); (2) short for a vulgarism meaning baloney or something less than the genuine article ("a bunch of B.S.").

BSA—short for Brigade Support Activity (such as the Drum and Bugle Corps and the cheerleaders), a variety of *ECA;* to midshipmen, the distinction can be significant: midshipmen in BSAs (as opposed to ECAs) may be excused from class, sports, and drill for BSA activities.

Bubblehead—a Navy-wide nickname for a submariner.

BUD/S—acronym for Basic Underwater Demolition/SEAL School, the *SEAL* basic-training center in Coronado, California; see *Mini-BUD/S.*

Budweiser—slang for the SEAL breast insignia; also a "bird."

Bulkhead—any wall (a Navy-wide term).

Bull Major—any of the Group III humanities majors (English, History, Economics, and Political Science), or any midshipman pursuing such a major; their exams tend to come late, and last, in exam periods.

Bust—(noun) a mistake; the condition of being wrong ("My bust" —that is, "My problem, my mistake, I was wrong"); (verb) to catch someone (or to be caught) doing something one shouldn't ("He got busted for coming in late").

Butter Bar—slang for the gold bars worn by ensigns and second lieutenants; by extension, also slang for those who wear them.

Buzz-Kill—a downer, a disappointing aspect, something sobering after an exhilarating high ("He got an A on the paper, so it was a real buzz-kill to learn that he got a D on the test").

BZ—see *Bravo Zulu.*

Cables—the level of electrical engineering taken by Group I majors; Group II and Group III majors take *Wires.*

Cadet—the name of midshipman counterparts at the United States Air Force Academy (USAFA) in Colorado Springs, Colorado, and at the United States Military Academy (USMA—West Point) in Highland Falls, New York, and at the United States Coast Guard Academy in New London, Connecticut; see *Plebe.*

Cake—from the phrase "a piece of cake": easy ("It was cake").

Camp Tecumseh—a derogatory nickname for the Naval Academy, largely used to describe Plebe Summer.

Canoe U—a nickname for the Naval Academy.

Capstone—a leadership course taken by Firsties in their final semester; the course follows *Service Assignment* and prepares midshipmen for their chosen career path.

Car—freedom.

Care Package—a box, usually from a sweetheart or home, usually containing food; sometimes called a "Share Package" or a "Chow Package."

Career Path—(1) one's path to this point in his or her career, or (2) the path projected (in terms of training and duty assignments) from this point; see *pipeline.*

Career Starter Loan—see *Second Class loan.*

Carrier Landings—running slides on the water-covered floors of Bancroft during Plebe Summer or Army Week; highly discouraged.

Carry-On—the privilege conferred on a Plebe to act normally; temporary freedom from Plebe rites and obligations ("He gave us carry-on at tables"); also a verb—to continue normal behavior, or to resume one's previous activity following an interruption.

CBDR—acronym for Constant Bearing, Decreasing Range: a collision course.

CDO—(1) abbreviation for Company Duty Officer—a First Classman who is head of a duty section in his Company; (2) abbreviation for Command Duty Officer—a commissioned officer assigned Main Office watch for a day (with the Officer of the Watch [OOW], a midshipman).

Chain—short for *chain of command.*

Chain of Command—(1) a Navy-wide term meaning administrative and operational channels; the superior-to-subordinate succession for commands; the subordinate-to-superior succession for requests; (2) the midshipman hierarchy (from Squad Leader to the Brigade Commander) or the military hierarchy (from Company Officer to the Superintendent—and beyond); common phrases are "Use the chain of command" and "Don't jump the chain."

Check Six—a military aviation phrase using clock-code direction terminology, short for "Check your six o'clock": that is, "Check what's behind you" or "Watch out" or "Be alert" or (in a crowd) "I've got your six" (meaning "I'm following right behind you").

Cherry—slang for a midshipman who has never been fried or in serious conduct trouble.

Chest Candy—slang for breast insignia, awards, ribbons, or any extra ornaments on uniforms.

SPECIAL REQUEST (Midshipman)				*(Use ballpoint pen or type.)*	

TO	From (Midshipman)			ALPHA NUMBER	
VIA	Class Year	Company	Room No.	Rank in Company	
REF. (a)	SQPR	CQPR	Last Apt.	Last Conduct Grade	

I RESPECTFULLY REQUEST (Type)
☐ Weekend Liberty ☐ Dining Out ☐ _____ Leave ☐ Other _____ (Specify)

Address (Care of) _____ (Street, P.O. Box, RFD) _____ (City) _____ (State) _____ (Phone)

Remarks or Reasons (if "DINING OUT," state with whom & relationship; "OTHER," explain.)

Signature (Midshipman)	Date	Beginning (Time & Date)	Ending (Time & Date)

SIGNATURE	DATE	APPROVED	DISAPPR'D	SIGNATURE	DATE	APPROVED	DISAPPR'D
Squad Leader				PRODEV			
Platoon Commander							
Company Commander							
Company Officer							
Battalion Officer							
Academic Dean (if required)							
Deputy Commandant				Departed (Time & Date)	Returned (Time & Date)		
Commandant				Signature (MCBO, MCMO, OOW)	Signature (MCBO, MCMO, OOW)		

NDW-USNA-BBA-1050/09 (Rev. 4-92)

A sample "Special Request Chit."

Chit—a written permission or excusal; examples are chits for late lights (for Plebes), for special liberty (special-request chits), or for excusing midshipmen from obligations such as classes or athletics because of injury or illness (medical chits).

Choke—(verb) to clutch or to tense up, and thereby (usually) to blow it.

Choker Whites—the formal summer uniform worn in most cases during the day (the nighttime version, the equivalent of a civilian tuxedo [or dinner jacket], is Dinner Dress Whites); see *uniforms.*

Chopping—the manner in which Plebes must move in Bancroft's halls and stairways; Plebes chop by taking short, double-time steps (about 160–80 steps per minute); chopping also consists of (1) moving along the center of all passageways (corridors) and along the outside bulkheads (walls) of all ladders (stairways), (2) squaring all corners, and (3) *sounding off* with motivational phrases such as "Go Navy, sir!" and "Beat Army, sir!"

Chow Calls—Plebe *rates;* 10 minutes and 5 minutes before breakfast and lunch if formations are inside (12 minutes and 7 minutes before those meals if formations are outside); Plebes quickly recite (1) where the formation is (inside or outside), (2) the uniform for the formation, (3) the menu for the meal, (4) the midshipman and officer on duty for the day, (5) the week's professional topic, and (6) the day's major events on The Yard; see *all-calls.*

Chow Package—see *care package.*

Cinderella Libs—*liberty* later than usual; from the long-time Navy-wide term for liberty ending at midnight (and the related "Sundowner Libs" for liberty ending at 6 P.M.).

Civilian—a day on which a midshipman has no classes; such days rarely are formally scheduled; more often, they occur via class cancellations and luck; see *Youngster.*

Civvies—(1) civilian clothes; (2) civilian-clothes privileges—i.e., the right to leave and return to the Academy in civilian clothes; civvies are generally enjoyed by all Firsties and Second Class going on, during, and returning from weekends or leaves.

CIWS (pronounced *see-wiz*)—acronym for Close-In Weapons System: the nickname for floor-fixed Bancroft door-holders, which resemble certain aspects of the close-in weapons system.

Classes—the Naval Academy classes, in order, are Fourth Class (Plebe), the counterpart of a freshman at a civilian college; Third Class (Youngster), a sophomore; Second Class (Second Class), a junior; and First Class (Firstie), a senior; see *Air Force Academy* and *West Point.*

Class Crest—designed for each class during Plebe year by a committee of midshipmen from that class; it appears on various wearing apparel, on the *class ring,* and on jewelry (available for purchase at the end of Plebe year) such as pins, necklace ornaments, cuff links, and tie tacks.

Classmate Loyalty—the concept or practice of looking out for one's own; sometimes generates conflicts with the *honor concept.*

Class Pictures—formal in-uniform color photographs taken of every midshipman every year, and usually available for purchase via mail by midshipmen and their families in time for Christmas; Plebes are photographed in Formal Dress Blues (*FDBs*); Youngsters are photographed in *choker whites,* and the yearbook picture (taken in Second Class year) must be in FDBs or chokers; N-winners may also be photographed in their letter sweaters.

Class Rank—see *Order of Merit.*

Class Ring—The Ring; the process of designing, selecting, and ordering begins at the end of Youngster year; since 1869 every class (except those of 1877–1880) has had its own design; not officially sanctioned on a midshipman's finger before the *ring dance;* worn with the class crest facing inward and the Academy seal facing outward until graduation, when the position is reversed; the ring is also made in a miniaturized form for giving as an engagement ring.

CMEO (pronounced *simeo*)—acronym for Command Managed Equal Opportunity: an Academy-wide effort, deriving from a Navy-wide program directed by the Chief of Naval Operations, (1) to see that all midshipmen have similar chances for leadership, and (2) to root out discrimination and prejudice; under CMEO the administration makes an annual cross-stratum climate assessment of such things as interviews, survey results, performance grades, and decisions of the *Academic Board;* CMEO appraisals also analyze demographic research conducted by the Academy's Department of Leadership and Law.

CMOD (pronounced *see-mod*)—acronym for Company Mate of the Deck, a Plebe or Youngster standing watch in a Company area; also called "the mate."

CMOOW—acronym for Company Midshipman Officer of the Watch, a Company Commander billet in Main Office under the *OOW.*

CNN Badge—the National Service Defense Medal, a ribbon sanctioned for midshipmen (and others) for being active-duty members of the armed forces during the 1991 Gulf War, which they watched via (primarily) CNN; also called "ketchup and mustard" because it is red and yellow; identical to the "alive in '65" badge given during the Vietnam War.

CO (pronounced *see-oh*)—(1) short for Commanding Officer, a Navy-wide term; (2) short for Company Officer.

Coast Guard Academy—in New London, Connecticut.

Coastie—a nickname for a student at the Coast Guard Academy.

COLEP—acronym for the mythical Company Laundry Exchange Program: lost laundry obviously has been requisitioned for participation in COLEP.

Colorado Country Club—a nickname for the Air Force Academy; also "The Bus Driver School."

Color Company—the Company with the most color points accumulated for everything from academics and athletics to parades and military activities; color points are awarded to stimulate rivalry among the Companies; the winning Company is honored during *Commissioning Week;* throughout the following academic year, midshipmen in the winning Company enjoy certain privileges—including the right to wear a gold E (for excellence) on their uniform.

Color Girl—usually the girlfriend or fiancée of the Company Commander of the *Color Company.*

Color Parade—a parade during *Commissioning Week,* at which the new *Color Company* is announced; the last parade for the First Class; see *Dedication Parade.*

Colors—the raising and lowering of the American flag; during Colors, midshipmen on The Yard face in the direction of the flag, stand at attention, and—if in uniform—salute for the duration of the ceremony; vehicles and pedestrians on The Yard are supposed to stop, as is the case at all military installations.

Come-Around—an instructional or training (or grilling) session for discipline or professional knowledge; a come-around involves a Plebe and an upperclassman, following which the upperclassman may sign a paper attesting to the Plebe's adequate performance and/or professional knowledge.

Commandant—the Academy's second-ranking military officer (after the Superintendent); essentially, the Commandant is the commanding officer of the midshipmen—overseeing health, welfare, discipline, and professional training; office is in Bancroft; also known as "the Dant."

Commandant's List—a midshipman makes the list with (1) an SQPR of at least 2.9, (2) at least a B in performance, (3) at least an A in conduct, and (4) at least a B in physical education; commonly called "the Dant's List"; see *Dean's List* and *Superintendent's List.*

Command Duty Officer—see *CDO.*

Commissioning Week—the week in late May culminating with graduation usually on May's last Wednesday; the week begins with the *Dedication Parade,* followed the same day by *Herndon;* both are a day before the *ring dance;* graduates receive B.S. degrees and commissions as Navy ensigns or Marine second lieutenants.

Company—the basic unit of organization within the Brigade, which has 36 Companies (6 per Battalion), each with about 120 midshipmen.

Company Commander—a First Class midshipman in charge of a Company.

Company Officer—a commissioned officer responsible for the training and military performance of a Company.

Company Wardroom—from the Navy-wide term for the officers' lounge/dining area aboard every ship; the Academy's equivalent of a civilian college's dormitory common room; located in a Company area, it usually has a TV, VCR, refrigerator, microwave, and other electronic amenities; most Academy wardrooms are sponsored by alumni classes; privileges to use a wardroom are conferred according to one's Academy class or academic status and are defined by Company policy as established by the Company Commander.

Comp Time—short for Compensatory Time; a canceled class, usually during *X-Weeks,* when a test in the same class is being given on the same day.

ComRats—a Navy-wide term for Commuted Rations: a credit entry in midshipmen pay accounts for meals served during authorized leaves; in other words, money returned to midshipmen for not eating in King Hall during vacations; see *MidRats.*

Conditioning Squad—a special-regime group for those midshipmen having trouble passing any part of the *physical readiness test (PRT);* see *PE deficient* and *sub squad.*

Conduct—(1) commendable behavior; (2) the Academy's system of administrative discipline (its official name: the Administrative Conduct System), which seeks to correct and educate rather than punish; the system evaluates midshipman behavior and adherence to regulations; midshipmen in conduct difficulty will likely find themselves receiving demerits, losing leave, serving *tours,* on *restriction,* or ultimately before a Conduct Board; appearance before such a board may result in *separation.*

Conduct Board—see *conduct.*

Con Locker—short for "confidential locker": the lockable locker in every midshipman's room.

Core Curriculum—required courses in engineering, the natural sciences, math, the humanities, and professional development; heavily weighted toward engineering, math, and science, the core curriculum constitutes the bulk of every midshipman's academic load; intended to ensure that every graduate is academically prepared to enter any Navy or Marine specialty.

Corfams—(often pronounced *cor-a-frams*): black synthetic-leather shoes, needing no wax (and permitting no foot to breathe); issued to all midshipmen.

Cork Off—(verb) to catch some quick rack time, to power-sleep.

Counseling—formal discussion ("He counseled me on how to make my rack").

The Countdown—the period beginning 36 days before *Herndon* when, on the day corresponding to its number (for example, the Fifteenth Company on the fifteenth day prior to Herndon), Plebes in each Company perform some outrageously ridiculous act.

Course Policy Statement—handed out on the first day of each course; written by the instructor, it gives information and guidelines regarding the course as well as the instructor's practices and expectations in his or her particular class; parts of a policy statement may be common among all instructors teaching a course with several sections; accompanied by a course syllabus.

Cover—(noun) a midshipman's cap, worn year-round since 1956; (verb) for one midshipman to indicate another's presence (accountability) at taps, lectures, or room visits ("Cover for me"); illegal.

CQPR (pronounced *c-kyooper*)—(also, phonetically, *kyoomie*): acronym for Cumulative Quality Point Ratio; see *GPA* and *Order of Merit.*

Crab—anyone, but usually a young woman, who lives in Crabtown.

Crabtown—a nickname for Annapolis; now used rarely by midshipmen.

Crank—(verb) to do well ("I really cranked on that test").

Crash and Burn—(verb) to perform poorly; to get the short end of the stick; to get hosed, to bite it, to die; to get shot down, as on a date.

Croquet—since 1982, the annual match with *St. John's.*

Cryppie—a member of the cryptology community.

CSORM (pronounced *see-sorm*)—acronym for Commandant's Standard Organization and Regulations Manual (incorporating what used to be known as *MidRegs,* formerly called "the Reg Book"): the bible of rules and regulations for midshipmen; contained in three-ring binders, it mirrors "the SORM"—the Navy's Standard Organization and Regulations Manual, a directive of the Chief of Naval Operations.

Cut (Me) Some Slack—(verb) give me a break; get off my case; see *slack.*

CWO—abbreviation for Company Watch Officer, a Firstie or Second Class who—on weekends—monitors midshipmen coming and going on leave, checking principally for alcohol.

Dad—see *Mom* (or *Dad*).

D&B—short for the Drum and Bugle Corps (sometimes called "the Drum and Bungle Corps"), formally established in 1925.

The Dant—short for the *Commandant.*

Dant's List—short for the *Commandant's List.*

Dark Ages—the period between Christmas and spring vacations.

Dark Side—from the movie *Star Wars:* a phrase connoting the dating of another midshipman ("He or she has gone over to the Dark Side"); see *Lima Victor.*

Dating—at the Academy (1) Plebes are permitted to date during *liberty* only; (2) no dating is permitted between midshipmen in the same Company or in a *chain of command* (if such a relationship develops, one of the participants may be moved); see *love chit.*

The Days—a Plebe *rate* consisting of the number of days to graduation, to the *ring dance* (four days prior to graduation), to the next leave period, and to the next Army-Navy athletic contest; the Days are often given in response to an upperclassman's demand, "Gimme the Days."

DB—short for Delta Bravo (or Beta) or *dirt bag.*

Dead Week—slang for the spring *Intersessional*—the week before *Commissioning Week.*

Dean—usually the Academy's Academic Dean and Provost, overseer of academics; sometimes another dean, either one of the foregoing's associates or the Dean of Admissions.

Dean's List—a midshipman makes the list in any semester with a semester QPR of at least 3.4 and no failures in any course or professional area; see *Commandant's List* and *Superintendent's List.*

Deck—a Navy-wide term for any floor or the ground.

Dedication Parade—a faculty-honoring parade that usually is the first official event of *Commissioning Week,* preceding *Herndon.*

Defense Language Institute (DLI)—at the Naval Postgraduate School, or *NPGS,* in Monterey, California.

Demerits—given on a sliding scale for a *fry,* which consists—singly or in combination—of *demerits, tours, extra duty,* and *restriction;* the elemental units of punishment measuring a midshipman's failure to use good judgment or to meet standards; demerits are used solely for determining semester conduct grades; also called "Demos."

Demos (pronounced *dee-mo's*)—see *demerits.*

Dental—in the basement of Bancroft's sixth wing; its services are available (and free) to all midshipmen, and every midshipman receives an annual screening—scheduled by Company.

DepDant—short for Deputy Commandant, the assistant to the Commandant.

Detailer—(1) a key player in determining every Navy officer's *career path:* any Washington-based officer designated to assist other officers with their duty assignments; found in the Bureau of Naval Personnel ("BuPers" or "Boopers"); the Navy equivalent of a Marine *monitor;* (2) a Second Class or First Class assigned to *Plebe Detail.*

Device—a Navy-wide term for insignia usually worn on the collars of uniforms.

Digger—a brown-noser; a *smack.*

Dining In—a formal, usually scripted, sit-down dinner such as one for a Company, team, or extracurricular group, and restricted to the group's members; see *dining out.*

Dining Out—a formal function, usually a dinner, for all the members of a Company, team, or extracurricular group and their non-Academy guests; see *dining in.*

Dirt Bag—a slime ball; a filthy or uncouth person; a poor performer.

Disco Dahlgren—an occasional term for a Saturday evening dance for upperclassmen in Dahlgren Hall; now rare.

Division I, Division II, Division III—the three groups of academic majors; Division I is engineering, Division II is science and math, Division III is humanities.

Dixie Cup—a midshipman's sailor hat; edged in blue and worn only by Plebes during Plebe Summer.

Dog It—(verb) to hold back, to give less than one's full effort—usually regarding something physical ("In the outer perimeter run, he dogged it all the way"); similar to *bag it.*

Dolphin—the submariner's breast insignia.

Doolie—see *Plebe.*

DOR—a Navy-wide acronym for Dropped, Own Request, wherein a participant in one mode of training requests—for whatever reason— transfer to another mode; whether justified or not, the assumption is often negative: i.e., that the participant made the request because of lack of aptitude or desire or because he or she found the training too tough.

Double Agent—an Academy graduate who ranks (or ranked) below 999 in his or her class; also a "secret agent."

Double-E—nickname for electrical engineering, notoriously one of the Academy's most troublesome courses, especially for *bull majors;* see *cables, wires,* and *single-e.*

Downstream—later, as in "See you downstream."

Downtown—Annapolis.

Drag—(1) a date; (2) a candidate for the Naval Academy visiting The Yard; (3) anyone taken to King Hall or around the Academy by a midshipman; (4) also a verb meaning to escort ("Are you taking a drag to the dance?" or "Are you dragging anyone?").

Dream Sheet—a Navy-wide term for any form filled out by midshipmen or officers regarding their desired career path.

Drill—parade practice; usually several times a week on Dewey, Farragut, or Worden Field for all midshipmen except in-season athletes, with additional practices for limited periods during the fall and spring; see *parades.*

The Driveway—a nickname for Turner Field, the synthetic grass field used for soccer, lacrosse, 150s football, and *PEP;* also called *"Turf Field."*

Drop—(verb) (1) to get down on the floor or ground, usually for push-ups; (2) to cease taking an academic course or to cease playing a sport ("I dropped English and squash"); (3) to rescind ("My fry was dropped"); see *DOR.*

Drunk Eagles—the situation occurring when the eagles on the side buttons on the side screws of a *cover* are crooked.

Drydock—a restaurant in Dahlgren Hall largely for midshipmen but also for visitors; see *Galley* and *Steerage*.

Dual Major—the taking of two majors, or one of the rare midshipmen doing so ("He's a dual").

Duty—see *on duty.*

Duty Section—the group of midshipmen in a Company on duty for a day, headed by the Company Duty Officer *(CDO);* from a Navy-wide term indicating that portion of a ship or squadron at duty stations and ready to react to emergencies.

Duty Station—a Navy-wide term indicating a place of assignment; see *station.*

ECA—acronym for Extracurricular Activity—any of about 100.

ED—abbreviation for *extra duty.*

EI—abbreviation for Extra Instruction; it is voluntary or mandatory, depending on academic status; a midshipman performing poorly in a class may be required to attend EI.

Eighth-Wing Players—an informal acting group, consisting primarily of midshipmen living in the Sixth Battalion, that gives lightly rehearsed humorous skits about Academy life in the eighth-wing parking lot on Thursday nights before home football games.

Eject—(1) to leave, or leave early; (2) to get out of a relationship.

E-Mail—short for electronic mail, the computer mailbox system on *NATS.*

EMI (pronounced *e-em-eye*)—a Navy-wide acronym for Extra Military Instruction: corrective instruction in cases of minor conduct infractions; not a punishment; usually for Plebes on Saturdays, and always approved by the Company Officer; its goal is to improve deficient performance in a specific phase of military duty—from how to wear a uniform properly to how to shine shoes, etc.; sometimes mistakenly equated with *extra duty.*

End-of-Semester Leave—the period in May between a midshipman's last exam and the beginning of the spring *Intersessional.*

Evolution—any activity that a midshipman has to do ("My next evolution, going to crew, is after lunch").

Exchange Student—any of up to 15 midshipmen who trade places with their counterparts at Air Force, West Point, and the Coast Guard Academy during the first semester of Second Class year.

Extra Duty—also called ED: duty that may be assigned by the administrative conduct system as punishment for a 4,000-, 5,000-, or 6,000-series conduct infraction, and to be carried out when the normal working day is over (usually on Saturday afternoons); ED may vary according to the discretion of the individual overseeing the punishment, but it ordinarily consists of non-fatiguing upkeep, maintenance, and administrative tasks in and around Bancroft; see *EMI* and *demerits.*

Excusal List—a list of those midshipmen released from an Academy obligation on The Yard because of special status (e.g., a BSA obligation); see *movement order.*

Eyes in the Boat—for Plebes, the act of keeping one's eyes set fixedly forward; a crew term; also a term from the days of sail, when ships' boats were powered by oarsmen forbidden to gawk at the passing scene.

Fac Rep—see *O Rep.*

Fair Winds and Following Seas—a Navy-wide phrase for "good luck" or "good sailing."

Fall Ball—out-of-season interscholastic scrimmages in lacrosse.

Farewell Ball—just prior to graduation during *Commissioning Week;* it dates from 1865.

Fat Blister—slang for a midshipman too overweight for a uniform; usually a low-performer in PE.

Fat Tables—slang for Battalion Double-Ration Tables: at breakfast and lunch, for varsity athletes bulking up; also "extra ration" tables.

FDBs—acronym for the Full Dress Blue uniform; see *uniforms.*

"Fidelity is Up, Obedience is Down"—(1) a Plebe *rate;* (2) a saying that confirms whether a watch belt is being worn right side up.

Fieldball—a rugged Academy intramural sport combining aspects of rugby, soccer, and lacrosse—and apparently played only at the Academy and at the New York State penitentiary.

Fighter Jock—slang for a fighter pilot.

First Class Alley—in King Hall, any aisle between the tables and the bulkheads (walls) where only Firsties may walk when going to and from *tables;* see *Second Class alley.*

First Class Cruise—a two-month cruise on a naval vessel (gray hull) in the summer prior to First Class year, for all those midshipmen not intending to select either Marines or *SEALs* as their warfare specialty; midshipmen wear khaki uniforms and live and work with junior-officer "running-mates."

First Class Parents Weekend—in September; the first semi-organized visit by parents since *Parents Weekend* at the end of Plebe Summer, and the last until *Commissioning Week.*

Firstie—a member of the First Class; the equivalent of a senior at a civilian college; see *Plebe, Youngster,* and *Second Class.*

Five and Dive—a slang phrase for serving one's five-year obligation after graduation and then leaving the naval service ("I'm gonna five and dive"); the term still holds, though the obligation is now six years.

Flamer—for the most part associated with Plebe indoctrination: an upperclassman who is excessively harsh on Plebes; taken from the verb "to flame," meaning to go off, to grill, to yell, or to scream ("He flamed on me at tables"); discouraged.

Flamer Stripes—slang for Second Class stripes; see *Flamer.*

The Fleet—the Navy and Marine Corps at large; the naval service; the real Navy.

Flyboy—a military-wide nickname for a pilot; often used derogatorily (some say) by those who couldn't qualify.

FMF—abbreviation for Fleet Marine Force—the Marines.

Formals—see *inspections.*

Formation—any assembling in ranks and taking a muster, but usually in reference to those formations prior to meals.

Form 2—a fry chit for being put on report; a paper filled out by the accuser when a midshipman does something supposedly not supposed to be done.

Forrestal Lecture—one of a series of addresses each year to the Brigade and public by a well-known speaker from outside the Academy; sometimes called by midshipmen a "Snorrestal Lecture" (from the verb "to snore") or a "Bore-us-all Lecture."

Forrest Sherman Field—(1) the formal name for Hospital Point, the area across Dorsey Creek and below the cemetery and hospital, containing playing fields and the *O Course;* (2) the home of the Blue Angels ("the Blues") in Pensacola, Florida.

40-Year Swim—a 40-minute swim test in the first semester of Second Class year; it is performed in khaki shirt and pants; those failing are put on the PE *sub squad.*

Foundation—short for the U.S. Naval Academy Foundation; its fundamental purpose is to arrange and sometimes help finance an additional year at college or prep school for Academy candidates in order to strengthen their academics prior to admission.

Four Years Together by the Bay—a phrase referring affectionately to midshipmen's years at the Academy; posted over the hall to Main Office; taken from the third verse of "Navy Blue and Gold" [see appendix for partial text].

Frat—short for *fraternization.*

Fraternization—a big no-no: (1) a Navy-wide term meaning undue familiarity within the *chain of command,* possibly resulting in special favors; (2) at the Academy, dating within a Company or the dating of an upperclassman and a Plebe (see *dating*); also, the condition wherein any upperclassman is too friendly with a Plebe.

French Out—(verb) a now-dated term for leaving The Yard without permission; see *Gate Zero* and *over the wall.*

Frog—slang for a pinch-clip for the spindle backs of uniform nametags and medals.

Fry—an indictment: its penalties are *demerits* and/or *restriction,* with a window for each depending on the nature of the offense; fries are issued in increments of 1,000, with 6,000 the most severe; also used as a verb, meaning to put (or be put) on report.

Fry Trap—a nickname for a restriction muster or any situation with especially high potential for disciplinary trouble; see *muster* and *NASP.*

FTN—abbreviation for a number of common phrases, one of which is "Fellowship Through Navy."

Funny Money—the running balance in their Naval Academy Store account that midshipmen never seem to see; put there via loans.

Galley—a restaurant in the Visitor Center primarily for tourists; see *Drydock* and *Steerage.*

Garrison Cap—the standard cover for the Navy khaki uniform; at the Academy, the pointed khaki hat worn only during the summer by upperclassmen on *Plebe Detail* and on cruise; often called a "fore-and-aft cap," a "piss-cutter," or a "banana cap"; see *uniforms.*

Gates—the Academy has three operating gates: Gate 1 (the Main Gate, sometimes called "The Visitors' Gate"), Gate 3, and Gate 8; each has a guardhouse and guards—enlisted Marines.

Gate Watcher—usually a *Bow Wow,* who stands at a gate on a Friday or Saturday night looking for infractions by returning mids.

Gate Zero—(1) an unused gate in the fence behind Halsey Field House; (2) the Wall, in the sense of going over it ("I used Gate Zero"); see *over the wall.*

Geek—one who studies all the time; a grind; see *gektoid.*

Geekers—eyeglass frames issued to all midshipmen requiring eyesight correction; often called, because of their effect on the opposite sex, "birth-control glasses."

Gektoid—hopelessly, extremely, forever a geek.

Get a Ride—regarding a Plebe: to win the privilege of not having to *chop* up or down stairways when accompanied by an upperclassman; also, "Give a ride": that is, for an upperclassman to do so.

Gig Line—the theoretical line made on a uniform by aligning the overlap of the shirt with the end of the belt and the overlap of the fly ("Jones, straighten your gig line").

Goat Court—either of two enclosed areas of Bancroft formed by Bancroft's third wing in the First Regiment and by Bancroft's fourth wing in the Second Regiment; the windows facing on the goat courts look onto a lower roof below; within the courts, noises echo seemingly forever.

GOOB—acronym for Going Out of Business: midshipmen leaving the Academy will often announce by Company chalkboard or by computer mail that they are having a GOOB sale to dispose of their Academy-related furnishings and belongings.

Gouge—(noun) assistance; the essential shortcut information on any subject; the answers; "previously acquired knowledge"; also used as a verb ("Gimme the gouge" or "Gouge me"); sometimes called "goo-hay"; gouge information from past tests and papers is illegal unless authorized by a professor or a department.

GPA—abbreviation for Grade Point Average (a.k.a. QPR); it averages academic grades only and is determined by (1) multiplying each course's grade (four points for an A, three points for a B, two points for a C, and one point for a D) by the number of credits for that course (the number of credits usually equals the number of hours the course meets each week), (2) adding those products, and (3) dividing that sum by the sum of the credits; see *CQPR* and *QPR.*

Grab-and-Go—a designated area of King Hall where midshipmen—usually upperclassmen, usually returning from athletic competition or practice—may get sandwiches, fruit, etc., for carryout at dinner time.

Grade Point Average—see *GPA.*

Graduation—the late-May day when midshipman *covers* are thrown into the air; what it's all about.

Graduation Salute—the first salute given by a new ensign or second lieutenant following *graduation;* by custom, the recipient of the salute receives a silver dollar.

Grape—a Marine term for the cranium or head ("Use your grape!").

Grappling—slang for the wrestling aspect of physical education for female midshipmen.

Gravy—the minute numerical fraction in a midshipman's SQPR or CQPR that makes him or her *sat* or *weekend eligible;* any small increment over the minimum.

Gray Hull—any Navy ship (surface or sub)—summer cruises on which are variously required of all midshipmen.

Grease—the best; (1) a midshipman's sharpest, crispest uniform or anything; (2) military aptitude—and any formal sit-down discussion between lowerclass and upperclass midshipmen, or between midshipmen and officers, to evaluate it; (3) a semester military evaluation of (a fitness report on) a midshipman's performance, attitude, officer potential, and leadership ability written by his or her superiors within the *chain of command;* (4) an adjective to describe a midshipman's best girlfriend or boyfriend, his or her one among many ("She's my grease girl"); also a verb (5) to oil the skids of one's own progress.

Green Beach—the outside edge of the roof of Bancroft, where midshipmen sometimes go, against regulations, to catch some rays; see *Red Beach.*

Grif—(verb) to *snarf* or steal (from the name of an individual named Griffin who deftly did so).

Grill—(verb) what a *flamer* does.

Ground Pounder—slang for an infantryman.

Gungy—from the Chinese (and Marine) gung ho: an adjective describing an overly motivated midshipman, one excessively psyched for the Academy or the Navy (or the Marines).

Hair—generally standard Navy regulations: (1) for men: after Plebe Summer (they are shaved on *I-Day*) hair must be tapered in the back and on the sides, and no longer than four inches on top; (2) for women: no hair-length requirement, but its bulk must not project more than 2 inches from the head, and women in uniform must wear their hair up and it must not impede the wearing of the *cover* (hat); barrettes must be brown or black; see *2-inch bulk rule;* (3) midshipmen are forbidden to give haircuts to other midshipmen; (4) hairpieces and limited Afros are legal.

The Hall—Bancroft.

Hall Rat—a midshipman who stays in Bancroft on weekends; one with limited, or no, social life.

Halo Effect—the benefits (or glow) deriving from a good first impression, thus charming the midshipman; there is also a "reverse halo effect."

Halsey Hack—a cough resulting from exercising—particularly from having run the *mile-and-a-half*—in Halsey Field House.

Hand to Gland—slang variation of "hand to hand," describing the self-defense training aspect of physical education for Second Class midshipmen.

Happiness Factor—the ratio of the number of days of a forthcoming leave to the number of days until that leave.

Harsh—(verb) to be difficult regarding, or tough on, another ("When I did it wrong, he really harshed on me").

Haze Gray and Under Way—assigned to sea duty on a ship: a Navy-wide glory phrase referring to (1) the actual or anticipated benefits of being an officer in the surface fleet; also (2) a real professional, one with lots of sea duty under his or her belt—applied most frequently to surface officers aboard haze-gray ships; see *SWO*.

Hazing—absolutely forbidden.

Head—a Navy-wide term for the toilet.

Head Shed—slang for headquarters; where the top officers hang out.

Head Restrictee (or Senior Restrictee)—the midshipman in charge of *accountability* at *restriction* musters; he or she is the midshipman with the most number of days served on restriction.

Heads-Up—probably from the baseball phrase, meaning "Look out!" or "Look alive!"; a bringing of something to someone's attention; a notification or warning ("I'll give you a heads-up when the stripers are in the Company area").

Height and Weight Restrictions—(1) 78 inches is the maximum height for commissioning; that standard may be waived, but anyone exceeding it usually faces limited service options; (2) any midshipman exceeding Navy weight standards may be dismissed.

Herndon—the symbolic end of *Plebe year,* and one of the first events of *Commissioning Week;* as a group, the Plebes scale the larded 21-foot granite Herndon Monument obelisk near the Chapel, and replace a glued-on blue-edged Plebe *dixie cup* hat with a midshipman's *cover;* at that moment Plebes technically become members of the Fourth Class—until donning their Youngster shoulder boards several days later at graduation (some contend that Fourth Classmen do not become Third Classmen until sighting the Chapel dome after their Third Class cruise); Herndon is formally called the "Plebe Recognition Ceremony"; informally, it is sometimes also called "T'ain't No Mo' Plebes."

High and Tight—the typical Marine (or infantry) haircut, consisting of closely cropped hair on top ("top" being defined as an extended hand) and nearly none on the sides.

High Speed, Low Drag—(1) a phrase describing something with many positive and few negative aspects; something cool ("Parking your car in the Supe's driveway is not high speed, low drag"); (2) its widely used shortened form ("high speed") is an expression meaning terrific, cool, sweet, or good news.

Hit the Wall—(verb) to reach one's point of exhaustion, as in an athletic event or in preparing for an exam ("On the weights, I hit the wall and couldn't do any more" or "In preparing for my double-e final, I hit the wall at 0400 and fell into the rack"); to be unable to do more.

HO—short for honor offense, essentially a violation of the *Honor Concept.*

Ho Chi Minh—from the Ho Chi Minh Trail in Vietnam: the tunnel labyrinth for the Academy's steam heating system.

Holidays—as federal employees, midshipmen receive federal holidays (Labor Day, Columbus Day, Veterans' Day, Martin Luther King Day, Presidents' Day); they also receive two days at Thanksgiving, two to three weeks at Christmas, and nine days (including weekends) for spring break.

Honor Committee—midshipmen representatives who investigate alleged honor offenses and make recommendations to the Commandant regarding their disposition.

Honor Concept—essentially, "Midshipmen will not lie, cheat, or steal" [see appendix for text]—a statement dictating any of three courses of action when a midshipman sees another lying, cheating, or stealing: (1) to counsel (that is, discuss the matter with) the transgressor and drop it, (2) to counsel the transgressor and turn the transgressor in, and (3) to turn in the transgressor without counseling; all counseling must be documented; *separation* is the principal sanction for an honor violation.

Honor Nazi—slang for any midshipman who is especially diligent in searching for honor offenses; see *reg hound.*

Hook—(noun) the preferred one, the one to get ("That class is the hook"); (verb) to give or receive assistance or the blessed benefit of the doubt ("Hook me on the math assignment" or "The prof hooked him with an A"); also "hooked up."

HOO-YAH!—the SEAL motivational call (or grunt); see *ARRU-GAH!* and *OO-RAH!*

Hop—(noun) any dance (formal or informal), usually at Dahlgren; (verb) to go over the wall ("He hopped the wall").

Hot Seat—at *tables,* the seat next to the Squad Leader—always occupied by a Plebe.

Hound—a monger; one constantly looking for something to an excessive degree, such as "a gouge hound" or "a reg hound."

Hospital Point—*Forrest Sherman Field.*

Hudson High—a nickname for *West Point.*

100s Night (formerly 100th Night)—the February night, 100 days from graduation, when for several joyous hours Plebes switch places with Firsties.

Ice Cream Suit—slang for a midshipman's short-sleeved Summer White uniform with shoulder boards; see *uniforms.*

I-Day—Induction Day, in early July; also referred to as "the hottest day of the year."

IHTFP—an acronym for several declarations common to midshipmen, three being "I Have Truly Found Paradise," "I Hate Those Friday Parades," and "I Have To Fly Planes."

Indoc—slang for the Fourth Class Development System, the system of professional development and indoctrination of Plebes.

Inner (or Outer)—(1) a run around The Yard's inner perimeter, about 3 miles; (2) a run around the inside of The Yard's outer perimeter, about 4.8 miles.

Inspections—among the many: personnel inspection (of a midshipman and his or her uniform at Company, watch, or restriction formation); haircut inspection; walk-through inspection (of midshipmen's rooms during the day or of midshipmen at formation); white-glove, black-sock formal room inspection (also called *formals* and *room formals*); and seabag inspection; the rooms of Plebes are generally inspected daily.

Intel—the intelligence community; see *spook.*

International Ball—a spring Brigade-wide dance, instituted by the Academy's foreign-language department, that draws foreign officers and embassy personnel and their young-adult children from the Washington, D.C., diplomatic community, as well as foreign-exchange students from nearby schools.

Intersessional—two periods of several days each, immediately prior to and following the spring semester, for in-class general military training; the spring Intersessional is the formal name for the weekend before *Dead Week.*

IP—short for *Irish pennant.*

Irish Pennant—from *Reef Points:* "an unseamanlike, dangling loose end of a line or piece of clothing"; hence, on a uniform, lint or loose thread suggesting lack of neatness.

Jacket—any file in any division or department containing records or information about a midshipman while at the Academy; the registrar permanently maintains all midshipman transcripts of grades; midshipmen retain their own medical and dental records, or jackets, upon graduation; all other jackets are destroyed two years following graduation.

Jarhead—a derogatory nickname for a Marine; in the presence of a Marine, should be used only by the smiling—or by SEALs; see *high and tight.*

Jet Jockey—a military-wide nickname for a jet (or fighter/attack) pilot.

Jewelry—watches are okay; discreet necklaces and religious medallions are okay if they cannot be seen when in uniform; rings are okay (limit: one per hand); anklets are not okay; bracelets and earrings are not okay for men; Navy uniform brushed gold-ball earrings (limit: one per lobe) are okay for women; love beads (trinkets) are not okay.

Jimmylegs—a widely used nickname for the United States Naval Academy Department of Defense police—those who provide security on The Yard; the Academy's equivalent of campus police; also called "the Legs"; also, a Navy-wide term for masters-at-arms, etc. (i.e., "the fuzz"); discouraged.

JO (pronounced *jay-oh*)—a Navy-wide term for junior officer: any officer new or comparatively new to the officer corps.

Joe Gish—see *W.T. Door.*

Johnny (or St. Johnny)—a student at *St. John's.*

Ju-Ju—vibes, karma, or deal; mystic togetherness; psychic hum; in most cases, not particularly good, indeed usually with the word "bad," as in: "The prof and I had bad ju-ju all term," or "The lacrosse team just couldn't get it together out there: bad ju-ju," or "Coming onto The Yard in civvies when you're supposed to be in uniform is bad ju-ju."

Kaydet—see *squid.*

King Hall—in Navy terms: the officers' mess, the equivalent of an officers' wardroom on a ship; where the midshipmen eat, in Squads (unless at *team tables*), 12 to a table; shaped in the form of a *T;* Plebes always face away from the *Anchor*—or away from the middle of the *T;* King Hall can feed the entire Brigade in several minutes.

Knockabout—a small sailing craft used by the Academy for instruction and recreation.

Labyrinth—the Academy's literary magazine.

Ladder—any stairway or set of stairs.

Late Lights—for Plebes, an hour extension, until midnight, with signed permission from their Squad Leader; see *lights out* and *taps.*

Leatherneck—(1) a military-wide nickname for a Marine; (2) a rigorous summer training option for rising Firsties interested in the Marine Corps; consists of several weeks at *The Basic School* and several with the Fleet Marine Force *(FMF);* sometimes called "Rubberneck."

Leave—authorization for extended absence from the Academy—notably for Thanksgiving, Christmas, Spring, and Summer vacations; leave generally begins after the last scheduled exam or military obligation; see *liberty.*

The Legs—see *jimmylegs.*

Liberty—a Navy-wide term for enlisted personnel (officers have "shore leave"); at the Academy it means authorization for midshipmen to depart Bancroft or *The Yard* for a comparatively short time (not more than 96 hours); liberty has several forms—notably *Yard liberty, town liberty,* and weekend liberty (for those not deficient in academics, physical education, conduct, or performance): (1) for the most part, liberty for Plebes is limited to town liberty on Saturdays and to Yard liberty on Sundays, though on certain occasions, assuming they are *weekend eligible,* they are granted overnight liberty; (2) Youngsters are granted three weekend overnight liberties each semester; they may depart on Saturday after the 10:15 A.M. liberty formation and must return by 6:00 P.M. on Sunday; (3) Second Classmen are granted six weekend overnight liberties each semester; they may depart on Saturday after the 10:15 A.M. liberty formation and must return by 6:00 P.M. on Sunday; (4) Firsties have unlimited overnight weekend liberties consistent with their obligations, and—like youngsters and Second Class—they may depart on Saturday after the 10:15 A.M. liberty formation and must return by 6:00 P.M. on Sunday; subject to periodic change, these were the stipulations governing weekends as of the time of publication; see *leave.*

Libs—short for *liberty* ("I've got libs this weekend").

Lid—slang for a midshipman's cap, or *cover.*

Lightning Rod—a *screen.*

Lights Out—for Plebes, at 11 P.M.; there are no lights out for upperclassmen; see *late lights* and *taps.*

Lima Victor—the phonetic-alphabet abbreviation for Lord Vader, from the movie *Star Wars:* the mythical embodiment of the temptations offered by midshipmen of the opposite sex; a female midshipman might say to her roommate, "Watch it, Kim. He's a Lima Victor"; see *Luke.*

The Limit—see *radius.*

Line Officer—a Navy or Marine commissioned officer eligible to succeed to command; Navy line officers wear a star on their sleeves above their rank insignia; First Class midshipmen wear a star on their sleeves even though they are not commissioned and are not line officers.

Load and Lock—(verb) from the command given to troops to load small arms; to get ready ("Hey. Load and lock. He's coming for inspection"); frequently said, in the wrong sequence, "Lock and Load."

Locked On—an adjectival phrase describing a midshipman who is extremely motivated and pro-Academy ("I didn't know you were so locked on that you would attend a softball game"); squared away; similar to *gungy.*

Log—a book or ledger for the recording of data or events during a watch.

The Log—the sometimes-published monthly midshipman humor magazine.

Lose Your Rear—(verb) to lose a bet, usually in reference to a Plebe; until released by the winning upperclassman, the losing Plebe must request permission to do practically anything, including sit down.

Love Chit—a *chit* submitted for moving a midshipman out of a Company to another because of a dating relationship within the original Company.

Lucky Bag—from the term for a ship's locker used for stowing miscellaneous confiscated, lost, or adrift items: the Academy yearbook, first published in 1894; reputedly the nation's largest, it contains highlights of the year plus pictures and hometowns of all graduating Firsties; all midshipmen are offered an opportunity to authorize the requisitioning of their pay to buy a copy; parents and/or guardians of Firsties receive forms to purchase their own; if purchased, it arrives by mail late in the fall following graduation.

Luke—as in Skywalker, from the movie *Star Wars:* any male midshipman contemplating dating a female midshipman; see *use the force.*

Main-O—short for Main Office, overseen by the Command Duty Officer *(CDO)* and assisted by the Officer of the Watch *(OOW)*—a midshipman three-striper or above.

Major—a midshipman's area of academic concentration, selected in the spring of Plebe Year; see *Division I, Division II, and Division III.*

Mameluke—a Marine sword—named for the hilt, or handle.

Mandatory—must do.

Mapper—slang for the acronym MAPR (Midshipman Academic Performance Report): a report of unsatisfactory progress from an instructor to a Company Officer regarding a midshipman receiving a D or an F in a course; in addition, all professors are supposed to write mappers for midshipmen scheduled for an *Academic Board* (such reports contain professors' evaluations of academic and military potential and may salvage or sink a midshipman before an Ac Board); formerly an "obit."

Mark 1 Mod 0 (pronounced *mark-one-mod-zero*)—the original version or model of something; now negative jargon for the genuine or official article, the basic goods; also, a preponderance of no-frills issue-gear ("Oooo. And here's my official Navy Mark 1 Mod 0 running shoe").

Marine—one of the few, the proud; midshipmen may choose to go either Navy or Marines, yet no more than 16 percent of a graduating class may select the Marines.

Marlinspike Seamanship—the art and science of tying nautical knots for practical or decorative purposes; also, non-engine sailboating, the variety the Academy teaches.

The Masqueraders—the Academy's drama club; the oldest Academy extracurricular organization, tracing its roots to 1849; said to be the nation's oldest collegiate theater group.

Mate—see *CMOD.*

Matrix—the computer grid or spreadsheet, generally based on a midshipman's major, showing his or her required courses, possible electives, course offerings, and vacant periods for the remaining semesters—a particularly important instrument during *pre-registration* and *registration;* the phrase (1) "she's ahead of her matrix" means that because of *validation* or transfer credits she has room to take an elective or a lighter load; (2) "behind the matrix" means a failed course that must be retaken and passed.

Max'd (or Min'd)—(verb) to receive the maximum (or mini-mum) punishment for a *fry* ("My Company Officer max'd me on my 4,000").

MCBO—acronym for Midshipman in Charge of Battalion Office—a Second Class.

MCMO—acronym for Midshipman in Charge of Main Office—a Second Class directing Plebes and Youngsters (generally *MOMs*).

Mech-E—slang for mechanical engineering ("I'm a mech-e"); widely regarded as one of the most difficult majors.

Medical—on Hospital Point near Gate 8: staffed 24 hours daily by medical personnel, with many visiting specialists; a full-service clinic, which sees patients by appointment or at *sick call;* all midshipmen receive free medical care and are given annual medical examinations; serious prolonged illnesses and injuries are often treated at Bethesda Naval Medical Center near Washington, D.C.; serious emergencies may be treated at Anne Arundel General Hospital and Medical Center in Annapolis, or in Baltimore.

Medal of Honor Room—any of numerous rooms in Bancroft named for Academy graduates who won the Medal of Honor.

Mem Hall—short for Memorial Hall; part of Bancroft; dedicated to Navy and Marine heroes and Academy alumni killed in combat (all of whose names are displayed); always a quasi-museum; formerly

OCEAN ENGINEERING MAJOR

CLASS OF 1996

Required Courses:

EM217	Strength of Materials	3-2-4	(1.0)
EN245	Principles of Ocean Systems Engineering	2-2-3	(1.0)
SO221	Intro to Oceanography	3-0-3	
EM324	Fluid Dynamics	3-2-4	(1.0)
EN380	Naval Materials Science and Engineering	3-0-3	(1.0)
EN441	Ocean Engineering Structures	3-0-3	(2.0)
EN461	Ocean Systems Engineering Design I	2-2-3	(3.0)
EN462	Ocean Systems Engineering Design II	1-4-3	(3.0)
EN475	Ocean Engineering Mechanics	3-2-4	(1.0)

Major Electives:

EN320	Microcomputer Aided Engineering and Design	2-2-3	(1.0)
EN361	Marine Power Systems	2-2-3	(1.0)
EN420	Coastal Engineering	2-2-3	(2.0)
EN430	Underwater Work Systems	3-0-3	(2.0)
EN440	Design of Foundations for Ocean Structures	3-0-3	(2.0)
EN450	Engineering Economic Analysis	3-0-3	(1.0)
EN470	Life Support Systems	3-0-3	(2.0)
EN477	Undersea Power Systems	3-0-3	(1.0)
EN479	Design of Floating Platforms	3-0-3	(3.0)

Other electives in Engineering, Science, Oceanography, Mathematics, and Computer Science upon approval of the Department Chair.

NOTES: HUM/SS electives, see page 7.

Engineering Design Requirements, see page 6. Numbers in parentheses indicate design credits.

Total design credits required	16.0
Available from required courses	13.0
Number required from electives	3.0

	THIRD CLASS		SECOND CLASS		FIRST CLASS	
C	NN200 3-2-4 NAVIGATION	NL202 2-0-2 LEADERSHIP II	NS310 1-2-2 TACTICS	NL302 2-0-2 LEADERSHIP III		NS401/2/3/4 1-2-2 JUNIOR OFFICER PRACTICUM
O	SM221 4-0-4 CALCULUS III	SM212 4-0-4 DIFFERENTIAL EQUATIONS		ES300 3-0-3 NAVAL WEAPONS SYSTEMS	ES410 3-2-4 CONTROL SYSTEMS	NL400 2-0-2 LAW FOR THE JUNIOR OFFICER
R	SP211 3-2-4 GENERAL PHYSICS I	SP212 3-2-4 GENERAL PHYSICS II	EE331 3-2-4 ELECTRICAL ENGINEERING I	EE332 3-2-4 ELECTRICAL ENGINEERING II		
E	HH205 3-0-3 WESTERN CIVILIZATION I	HH206 3-0-3 WESTERN CIVILIZATION II				
COGNATE			3-0-3 HUM/SS ELECTIVE			3-0-3 HUM/SS ELECTIVE
COGNATE			EN319 3-0-3 ENGINEERING THERMODYNAMICS		FREE ELECTIVE 3-0-3	
COGNATE	EM211 3-0-3 STATICS	EM232 3-0-3 DYNAMICS	EM217 3-2-4 STRENGTH OF MATERIALS	EM324 3-2-4 FLUID DYNAMICS		
M A J O R		EN245 2-2-3 PRINCIP OF OCEAN SYSTEMS ENGR	EN380 3-0-3 NAVAL MAT SCIENCE AND ENGINEERING	EN441 3-0-3 OCEAN ENGINEERING STRUCTURES	EN475 3-2-4 OCEAN ENGINEERING MECHANICS	MAJOR ELECTIVE 3-0-3
M A J O R				SO221 3-0-3 INTRODUCTION TO OCEANOGRAPHY	EN461 2-2-3 OCEAN DESIGN I	EN462 1-4-3 OCEAN DESIGN II
M A J O R					MAJOR ELECTIVE 3-0-3	MAJOR ELECTIVE 3-0-3
	18	19	19	19	17	16

TOTAL SEMESTER HRS: 142
MAJOR: 31

A sample matrix for a class of 1996 ocean engineering major (from "The Majors Program").

the site of Plebe swearing-in ceremonies, "tea fights," and—before the acquisition of the Alumni House—Alumni Association annual dinners; now the site of various Academy functions, symposiums, and retirements; demands solemn, respectful conduct; hats are always removed except those of midshipmen on watch such as the *BOOW.*

Merchant Marine Academy—in King's Point (Long Island), New York.

Mess Night—a practice formal dinner held in the spring of Second Class year—featuring, among others, the "President of the Mess" and "Mr. Vice."

Mice—real ones: Bancroft's longest, most adaptable, most tenacious residents; catching them ranks among the midshipmen's most relentless pursuits; upon catching five, a midshipman becomes an "ace."

Micromanager—someone who has to oversee every detail of a project; generally synonymous with Company Officer; also, sometimes, "picomanager."

Mid (Mids)—short for midshipman (midshipmen); acceptable terms; see *middy (middies).*

Middy (Middies)—unacceptable nicknames for midshipmen, particularly the latter form; those who know don't use the terms; see *mid (mids).*

Mid Hawk—a non-midshipman female (or male) looking for a male (or female) midshipman to date; also known as *squid bait.*

Mid Hunter—synonym for *mid hawk.*

Midiot—any midshipman not exercising the full capacity of his or her brain.

Midn—common written abbreviation for midshipman.

MidRats—short for Midshipmen Ration Allowance: (1) box lunches; (2) dining hall meals for those coming off watch; see *ComRats.*

MidRegs—short for Midshipmen Regulations, formerly the bible of disciplinary rules governing midshipman life; now incorporated into *CSORM.*

Midshipchick—occasional slang for a female midshipman.

Midshipman—the term applied to all students at the Naval Academy; it dates from the British navy in the late 17th century, when young men training to be officers were frequently assigned to stations on the deck about midway between the bow and stern, probably so they couldn't get in the way; midshipmen are not officers of the line (see *line officer*), but most become so upon commissioning at graduation; midshipman caps, which midshipmen throw into the air at graduation, feature a fouled anchor (with line wrapped around it), whereas the anchor on officers' and chiefs' caps is not fouled.

Midshipman Activities Center—a lounge upstairs in Dahlgren Hall.

Midshipman Welfare Fund—with monies derived from the Naval Academy Store, the fund largely finances *ECAs* and social functions.

Midslang—the Naval Academy vernacular.

Midspeak—the language peculiar to midshipmen; often a derogatory term employed by midshipmen in reference to other midshipmen who speak too much like midshipmen.

Mid Store—see *Naval Academy Store.*

Mile-and-a-Half—a run for time required of all midshipmen every semester; it usually is conducted outside on the Ingram Field track—except in winter or in bad weather, when it is conducted in Halsey Field House (thus inducing the *Halsey hack*); women must run it under 12 minutes 40 seconds, men under 10:30.

Milfacts—a Naval Institute computer file, accessible by all midshipmen, containing a vast amount of information about military matters.

Miltex—at the Academy, toilet paper; also known as sandpaper and John Wayne toilet paper.

Miniature—a small copy of the *class ring* given as an engagement ring.

Mini-BUD/S—a summer-option four-week taste of *BUD/S* for those rising Firsties thinking of the *SEALs* as a warfare specialty.

MIR—abbreviation for Midshipmen in Ranks: Firsties graduating later than their class; in addition, many Company billets are *MIR* (such as wardroom rep, academic officer, drill officer, etc.).

Misery Hall—the health/trainer areas of Macdonough Hall, Halsey Field House, and the eighth-wing varsity locker room where damaged athletes go for rehabilitation and repair.

Mo Board—polar-coordinate graph paper used in some navigation and leadership courses and on *YPs* ("mo" is short for "maneuvering"); used extensively in the *fleet* to compute ship movements—e.g., to determine the distance between passing ships.

MOM (pronounced *mom*)—acronym for Main Office Messenger, a Plebe.

Mom (or Dad)—a Company Officer overly on a midshipman's case.

Monitor—the Marine equivalent of a Navy *detailer.*

Monterey—short for the Naval Postgraduate School (or the PG School) in Monterey, California, where Academy graduates and other officers go for advanced study—but rarely right after graduation from the Academy; see *NPGS.*

Morning Quarters—before-breakfast accountability (attendance) formations in Company areas to pass the word; follows *officer's call.*

Mother B—an increasingly dated nickname for Bancroft.

Movement Order—a listing of those midshipmen authorized to participate in a special event outside The Yard; to make a movement order, a midshipman must have a 2.0 GPA; see *excusal list.*

MPO—acronym for Mustering Petty Officer, an attendance-taker at formations or taps, usually a Second Class; see *section leader.*

MPS—acronym for Midshipmen Pay Statement: received monthly by midshipmen, spelling out their earnings, charges, withholding, and deductions.

Mrs. Supe—the *Supe*'s wife.

Multiple Guess—slang for a multiple-choice test.

Muster—(1) a roll call or a formal taking of attendance (accountability): for meetings, taps, formations, etc.—usually in ranks; (2)

a restriction muster: a requirement, as punishment, for midshipmen on *restriction* to assemble at a designated time in inspection-ready uniform.

Mutiny—the condition declared when an upperclassman discovers more than four Plebes in a room: the Plebes go into the shower with their clothes on; exception: a mutiny cannot be declared if the room contains an American flag.

NAAA—or the N-Triple-A (for Naval Academy Athletic Association), which organizes, promotes, and variously assists with Academy athletic programs.

NAFAC—acronym for the annual week-long Naval Academy Foreign Affairs Conference; held in the spring, it attracts prominent speakers and college students from across the country.

NAMI—acronym for Naval Aeronautical Medical Institute, which is the final approval authority on aviation exams: by extension, the eye test prospective aviators take in Pensacola; because of the high failure rate, known widely as the "NAMI Whammy."

NAPS—acronym for the Naval Academy Prep School in Newport, Rhode Island; about 200 midshipmen annually enter the Academy from the one-year NAPS program; also, the Naval Academy Primary School in Annapolis.

NAPSter—anyone attending (or a midshipman who attended) NAPS—the Naval Academy Prep School; often called a "Hamster."

Narc—(noun) short for naval architecture, or for a midshipman majoring in it; (verb) to turn someone in to the authorities ("He narc-ed me").

NASP—acronym for Naval Academy Summer Programs: the entity that oversees all midshipmen at the Academy during the summer (except Plebes and those on *Plebe Detail*); those under NASP are primarily midshipmen attending summer school; NASP often has a number of recent Academy graduates who are on *TAD;* widely regarded as possibly the Academy's biggest *fry trap.*

NASS—abbreviation for the Naval Academy Sailing Squadron, headquartered in the Robert Crown Sailing Center.

NATS—acronym for Naval Academy Time-Sharing System—the Academy's computer information/mail system accessible throughout The Yard; often NADN, for Naval Academy Data Network.

Nav—short for any navigation course; the Academy requires a course in coastal piloting, shiphandling, and celestial navigation for graduation.

Naval—a collective adjective referring to the Navy and the Marine Corps; "naval" officers are both Navy and Marine officers.

Naval Academy Store—midshipmen still often call it by its former name, the Mid Store; the Academy's campus store, where midshipmen shop; it contains everything from books to watches, stereos to snacks, as well as a superabundance of Navy/USNA clothing, mugs, bumper stickers, etc.; nearly $1 million of its profits help fund *ECAs* and club sports; visitors must be accompanied by a midshipman or by other Navy personnel; hours are 7:30 A.M. to 3:30 P.M. Monday through Friday, and 7:30 A.M. to noon on Saturday; closed on Sunday, during certain vacation periods, and on Saturday in the summer.

The Naval Service—the fleet; the Navy at large—including the Marines.

Navy Flight School—in Pensacola, Florida.

Negative—military-wide term for "no"; see *affirmative.*

Negatory—a military-wide term for *negative* or no.

Net Pay—what's left.

NFO—acronym for Naval Flight Officer (either Navy or Marine): an individual usually *NPQ,* usually because of below-grade eyesight—thus ineligible to be a pilot; also, interchangeably, a "backseater" and—variously—a "bombardier/navigator (BN)," a "tactical contact coordination officer (TACCO)," and a "radar intercept officer (RIO)."

NHS—acronym for the Naval History Symposium, held every other fall under the sponsorship of the Academy's Department of History.

Ninth Wing—generically, any apartment, apartment complex, or other housing used by recent Academy graduates on *TAD* while they await the beginning of their first service assignment; specifically, an apartment complex several miles from the Academy; also, the moment's most popular nightspot in town.

NLT—abbreviation for "not later than."

The Nod—(1) the affliction of sleepy midshipmen; most professors will allow midshipmen about to nod off to stand up in the back of the room and continue to take notes; (2) approval, the go-ahead ("Did Lt. Jones give you the nod?").

Non-Reg—short for "non-regulation": see *un-reg.*

NPGS—abbreviation for the Naval Postgraduate School in Monterey, California; also called "the PG School."

NPQ—see *PQ.*

NPS—abbreviation for the Nuclear Power School, in Orlando, Florida.

Nugget—anyone new to a unit or group, especially an aviation squadron.

Nuke—a nickname for anyone in nuclear power, usually a submariner; an officer on a surface nuclear ship is often called a "Surface Nuke"; also sometimes used to connote a by-the-book mentality.

OAO—acronym for several phrases, including "one and only," "off and on," and "one among others."

Obligation—one's service commitment: used often in reference to the number of contract years to be served in the Navy or Marines following graduation; the obligation is five following graduation except: (1) for naval aviators it is seven years after the earning of their wings, and (2) for those taking graduate degrees the obligation is usually lengthened by two years for every year of funded graduate education.

OBSTCR (pronounced *ob-sticker*)—acronym for "or be subject to conduct report," meaning "do this or else"; like *ASAP,* often attached to messages.

Ocean-E—short for ocean engineering: courses in it, the major, or midshipmen majoring in it.

O Club—short for the Officers' and Faculty Club; also, sometimes, the O&F Club; has 3,200 dues-paying members; midshipmen may use the club under various circumstances—as may their parents at just about any time.

O Course—short for the Hospital Point obstacle course, 490 yards and 13 obstacles, used principally during *Plebe Summer.*

ODEWS—acronym for the mythical OD Early Warning System: when "Attention on Deck!" is shouted by the mate or the first person to notice the presence in the area of an officer, usually a commander or above; by extension, any system for giving early or advance announcement of an officer's arrival.

Office of Legal Counsel (OLC)—in Mahan, an office that provides midshipmen with legal assistance and advice; in certain cases, the OLC counsel may act as the lawyer for, or defender of, a midshipman in discipline trouble—and in such cases a member of the Department of Leadership and Law may act as an impartial investigator, provided the member of the OLC has not had the midshipman as a student.

Officer's Call—(1) a before-breakfast meeting at which the Company Commander or Sub-Commander briefs the nine Squad Leaders and three Platoon Commanders on the day's important announcements; at the subsequent *morning quarters,* the Squad Leaders and Platoon Commanders then repeat the announcements to the Squads; another way for getting information to the *Brigade;* (2) that part of a parade when all the officers and guidon bearers assemble and salute the Brigade Commander.

Officers' Club—see *O Club.*

"Oh Shit!" Hill—the first hill on Maryland Rt. 450 north of the Naval Academy Bridge; it gets its name from the exclamation of some midshipmen as they crest the hill upon returning from liberty or leave, and see the Naval Academy before them.

OLC—abbreviation for the *Office of Legal Counsel.*

On Duty—on a daily watch or serving in one's Company's rotational weekly duty section, such as the *OOW* or *MCBO.*

1/C—standard written abbreviation for First Class midshipman; also, 2/C (Second Class), 3/C (Third Class), and 4/C (Fourth Class).

1-MC (pronounced *one-em-cee*)—the Bancroft speaker system, used for announcing formations, the weather, and uniforms for the day.

1-90 (pronounced *one-tac-90*)—an anti-hazing regulation prohibiting any abusive behavior, particularly by upperclassmen toward Plebes; an adjunct is the stipulation that no midshipman may touch another without his or her consent—except when adjusting uniforms and in approved contact sports.

On Report—having one's name sent to the administration for an alleged infraction ("I'm on report for being late for taps"); synonymous with "I'm fried."

OOM—acronym for *Order of Merit.*

OO-RAH!—the Marine motivational call (or grunt); also ARRU-GAH!; see *ARRUGAH!* and *HOO-YAH!*

OOW—acronym for Officer of the Watch, the highest-ranking watch billet for a midshipman; the only midshipman who rates a salute from another midshipman; see *CDO.*

ORB—acronym for the Objectives Review Board, the Superintendent's top advisory board.

Order of Merit—(also OOM): class rank; a midshipman's rank in his or her class; a combination of one's academic (65 percent) and conduct and military performance (25 percent), plus grades for physical education, athletics, and the *PCR* exam; all grades are multiplied by predetermined coefficients, and the consequent numbers are totaled—resulting in an aggregate multiple; that multiple is then translated into a Cumulative Quality Point Ratio (CQPR, or—phonetically—*kyoom* or, more affectionately, *kyoomie*) and a Semester Quality Point Ratio (SQPR); offshoots are (1) one's Academic Quality Point Ratio (AQPR) or simply one's Quality Point Ratio (QPR, one's current Grade Point Average [GPA]), and (2) one's Military Quality Point Ratio (MQPR).

O Rep (or Fac Rep)—for Officer Representative (or Faculty Representative): an officer or civilian faculty member assigned to an athletic team or an extracurricular group (some teams have one of each); the team's or group's link(s) with the Academy administration; mentors, supporters, "friends in court."

Orientation Day—in mid-May, a preliminary glimpse for Academy candidates offered appointments.

Ortho—the part of *Medical* for orthopedic injuries.

Outer—see *inner.*

Overhead—a Navy-wide term for any ceiling, or any lights in a ceiling; the underside of the above *deck.*

Over the Side—(1) a synonym for *over the wall;* (2) a phrase usually used with the verb *go:* separating, or leaving the Academy; punching out.

Over the Wall—used variously with the verbs *jump, hop,* or *go:* the act of leaving (or entering) The Yard without permission; also, out when you're not supposed to be; see *Gate Zero.*

"Over the Wall!"—a computerized electronic bulletin board operated by the Alumni Association; intended for use by (among others) parents' clubs and parents of midshipmen; accessible by dialing 800-982-USNA.

Parades—a major part of Brigade life; there are formal parades, on Worden Field, and practice parades; see *drill.*

Parents Weekend—at the end of Plebe Summer; frequently the first parental (etc.) glimpse of a midshipman after *I-Day;* occasionally called "Plebe Parents Weekend"; see *First Class Parents Weekend.*

Passageway—a Navy-wide term for any hallway or corridor used for horizontal movement.

PCR—abbreviation for Professional Competency Review; tests given annually in late winter, covering all the professional knowledge a midshipman is expected to have mastered since Plebe Summer; midshipmen must take the test repeatedly until passing it; those encountering difficulty on the test face mandatory PCR *EI;*

every midshipman's performance on the test becomes part of his or her military grade and thereby is factored into his or her *OOM.*

PE—(1) abbreviation for Physical Education; all midshipmen must take PE each semester and must pass tests in the various required athletic activities; see *pre-test* and *validate;* (2) abbreviation for graded Practical Exercises in navigation courses; PEs are usually given in the evening and last several hours.

Pecker—a nickname for any *Professional Competency Review (PCR)* test.

PE Deficient—a midshipman failing to meet any physical-education standard is deemed PE deficient; he or she is assigned to a *conditioning squad* or *sub squad,* where he or she works toward meeting the standard; those not meeting the standards face *separation.*

Pencil Neck—a number-cruncher; a *geek.*

Pentagram—a nickname for the Pentagon; also a Pentagon message or document.

PEP—acronym for Plebe Summer's Physical Excellence Program (Plebes often call it the "Plebe Exhaustion Program"); consisting of early-morning calisthenics on the synthetic grass field and runs around The Yard, PEP is designed to condition Plebes to the Brigade's physical standards.

Pep Rally—mandatory fun.

Performance—evaluation of professional duties; a military ranking among the midshipmen within a Company every semester; the ranking is determined by (1) the Company's *stripers,* who use information from other upperclass midshipmen within the Company (midshipmen grade those in the classes below them), and by (2) the Company Officer; this ranking (or grade) plays a large role in a midshipman's performance grade, which appears on his or her semester grade report and becomes part of his or her *OOM.*

Performance Board—a board that considers reported cases of substandard military performance by midshipmen.

Performance Grade—see *performance* and *OOM.*

Personal Services—a department in the Naval Academy Store; it offers everything from photocopying and video rental to film developing and gift wrapping.

PG School—see *NPGS.*

Phone Room—any of numerous pay-telephone areas in Bancroft.

Phone Home—(verb) from the movie *E.T.:* regarding Plebes, to get in the shower during Plebe Summer with one's clothes on and (for "practice") to turn the shower knob in simulated dialing of a telephone; discouraged.

Physical Education—see *PE.*

Physical Readiness Test (PRT)—a graded semester test required of all midshipmen and consisting of stipulated numbers of push-ups and sit-ups, plus passage of the sit-and-reach flexibility test.

Piece—a non-functioning, fused-bolt rifle used for midshipman *drill.*

Ping—(1) a high-stepping, arms-turned-up, form of *chopping* no longer in use; (2) as a verb, to scout for the opposite sex; (3) phonetic acronym for *pencil neck geek.*

Pipe—(verb) to shaft, hose, or *slam.*

Pipe Down—(noun) the completion of duty or watch activities; (verb) to go off duty or watch.

Pipeline—the likely future path within a warfare designation—the training schools a midshipman will attend after graduation, their location, etc.; see *career path.*

Plates—short for "deckplates": metal squares on the floors of Bancroft corridors at major *chopping* intersections where Plebes turn, *square their corners,* and *sound off;* a common phrase—a takeoff on a quote by World War II Admiral Bull Halsey—is: "Hit the plates running—hit ['em] hard, hit ['em] fast, and hit ['em] often."

Platform—a Navy-wide term for any surface ship, submarine, or aircraft used to launch ordnance.

Platoon—a unit of organization within the Brigade; there are three Squads per Platoon, and three Platoons per Company.

Platoon Commander—a two-striper midshipman; see *Platoon.*

Plebe—from the word "plebeian"—a commoner, or, in the modern vernacular, a low-life: (1) a member of the Fourth Class; the equivalent of a freshman at a civilian college; see *Youngster, Second Class,* and *Firstie;* (2) at West Point, Plebes are "Plebes"; at the Air Force Academy they are "Doolies."

Plebe Cut—for men, shaved; for women, short; see *hair.*

Plebe Detail—the contingent of upperclassmen, in either of two *sets,* assisting with training Fourth Class inductees during *Plebe Summer;* often called "Detail."

Plebe Indoc—see *Indoc.*

Plebe Informal—a very occasional dance.

Pleber—a nickname for a Plebe.

Plebe Recognition Ceremony—the official name of *Herndon;* also called the "T'Ain't No Mo Plebes" ceremony.

Plebe Summer—the opening ordeal, the beginning of the Naval Academy experience; a giant *come-around;* from generally the first week of July through the third week of August; see *Real Plebe Summer.*

Plebe Summer Smell—the blended aroma of new uniforms, issue-gear, anxiety, and sweat; the smell unique to Plebe Summer and remembered by all midshipmen and Academy graduates.

Plebette—a nickname for a female Plebe; discouraged.

Plebe Year—the end of the beginning, officially concluded by the scaling of *Herndon* on the first day of *Commissioning Week.*

POD (pronounced *pee-oh-dee*)—a Navy-wide acronym for the Plan of the Day: the posted bulletin of daily activities at the Academy and on The Yard, and giving notice of future events.

PQ (or NPQ)—abbreviation for Physically Qualified (or Not Physically Qualified), as determined primarily by pre-commissioning physicals *(pre-comms);* if a midshipman is designated NPQ, he or she cannot serve as an unrestricted-line officer.

PQS—acronym for Personal Quality Standards: an officer's book of accomplishments following commissioning; at the Academy, a PQS is a book used for watches and for Plebes in their second semester; a Plebe gets someone already proficient at a task to "sign off"—to sign the book, thereby vouching for his or her proficiency at that task.

P-rade—short for *parade.*

Pre-Comms—pre-commissioning physicals for midshipmen; detailed and on-going, they begin in the second semester of Second Class year and may continue through *Service Assignment* and until graduation.

Pre-Registration—see *registration* (or *pre-registration*).

Presidential Pardon—the tradition that on visits to the Naval Academy, the President or a foreign head of state pardons certain midshipmen on *restriction* at that time—as well as those with outstanding *conduct* or *performance* offenses; also called "amnesty."

Pre-test—a procedure whereby midshipmen, notably members of varsity athletic teams, attempt to pass a test (or *validate*) early to satisfy their *PE* or *PRT* requirement.

Prior—short for midshipmen who were "prior enlisted"—that is, those who came to the Academy from the Navy fleet or from the Marines ("He's a prior").

Priority—the condition of being eligible (primarily varsity athletes and midshipmen either at risk or with high academic standing) for early sign-up for specific courses and sections; on varsity teams, those with the lowest CQPRs usually receive the highest priority.

Probation—in most cases, an alternative to *separation;* restricted privileges (such as denial of weekends) because of deficiencies in academics, performance, conduct, or PE ("I'm on probation"); the message to midshipmen on probation: improve.

Probes—slang for *probation.*

Pro Book—a paperback containing information on military subjects; used in the first semester of Plebe Year; the second semester, Plebes get a *PQS* book; Plebes, and ultimately all midshipmen, are responsible for knowing the information in pro books and related *professional* material; see *PCR, professional knowledge,* and *pro topic.*

ProDev—short for Professional Development: the Academy division that coordinates professional training during the academic year, as well as *summer training;* located on the third floor of Luce Hall.

Prof—short for professor; the term used by all midshipmen to refer to all Academy teachers.

Professional—an adjectival near-synonym for "military" and/ or "naval," as in "professional knowledge" or "professional development."

Professional Competency Review—see *PCR.*

Professional Knowledge—(also Pro Knowledge): (1) part of Plebe training: information about military matters, ranging from uniforms to enemy armament (see *pro topic*); (2) all midshipmen are tested annually on their accumulated learning in *professional* areas (see *PCR*).

Pro Flick/Pro Lecture—movies or lectures for Plebes—generally on Saturday mornings, generally related to the week's *pro topic.*

Pro Report—an in-depth report given by Plebes, usually to Plebes, on a given *pro topic;* now generally given for *EMI.*

Pro Topic—the professional subject under study for a stipulated period (usually a week), during Plebe Summer and Plebe Year; such topics are delineated in Plebe *pro books,* covered in Plebe reference manuals, reinforced in *pro flicks* and *pro lectures,* and tested in pro quizzes or pro tests (on Friday afternoons, with makeups on Sundays)—as well as discussed at meals by Plebes in pro reports; see *PCR* and *pro book* and *professional knowledge.*

PRT—abbreviation for *Physical Readiness Test.*

PT—abbreviation for Physical Training: any physical exercise— organized or un- ("I'm going out for some PT'").

Puddle Pirate—a nickname for a member of the Coast Guard.

Puke—a disreputable person; a jerk; a *dirtbag.*

Punch Out—(verb) from the aviation phrase meaning to eject: to separate or disenroll—i.e., leave the Academy; also "to punch" ("He was having a tough time, so he punched").

Puzzle Palace—a nickname for the Pentagon.

P-way—short for *passageway.*

QPR *(kyooper)*—acronym for Quality Point Ratio; see *Order of Merit.*

Rack—(noun) a bed; (verb) to sleep.

Rack Attack—an overwhelming need to sleep.

Rack Monster—a mythical animal that grabs midshipmen and throws them into bed ("The rack monster got me"); the best excuse for why one misses a class.

Rack Option—the right of Plebes to go to bed at 10:00 P.M.

Rack Races—*Plebe Summer* practices designed (1) to promote familiarity with making one's bed, and (2) to promote speed in doing so; see *uniform races.*

Radar—the gold band on a *cover* ("Your radar is up").

Radius—the distance from the Academy (22 miles) beyond which a Plebe or Youngster (1) may keep and/or drive a car, and (2) wear *civvies;* sometimes called the "liberty radius" and "the limit."

Rate—(noun) designated military (or *professional*) information a Plebe is required to know; (verb) to merit or qualify for; to be entitled to by class or rank ("Plebes do not rate that" or "You rate knowing this").

Rate What You Skate—(verb) to do what you can get away with until you get caught.

Ratey—from the verb "to rate": an adjective ordinarily employed in reference to Plebes who assume privileges they are not normally permitted: for example, those who slouch at tables, say, "Sir" too infrequently, or generally act insufficiently subordinate; an upperclassman's observation might be, "So-and-So is ratey."

Real Plebe Summer (or Year)—the last tough one, usually the one experienced by the speaker; see *Plebe Summer* and *Plebe Year.*

Recon—a spirit-promoting after-hours venture of Plebes and (sometimes) upperclassmen; officially discouraged.

Red Beach—any of the red-tiled areas at the back of Bancroft and above King Hall where midshipmen catch rays; see *Green Beach*.

Red Time—during Plebe Summer, a period before lunch when upperclassmen are not allowed to occupy Plebes.

Reefer—a short three-brass-button black winter coat for classes (the officers' version of the sailors' pea-coat); longer than a campus jacket (now not used) and shorter than a four-button overcoat; with the addition of officers' shoulder boards, an officer's uniform item.

Reef Points—(1) since 1905, an annually published manual for Plebes, practically their Plebe Summer bible; (2) from *Reef Points:* "pieces of small stuff used to reduce the area of a sail in strong winds, making for smoother sailing"—hence, helpful tidbits of information.

Regiment—a unit of organization within the Brigade, which has two Regiments—First and Second (or, during *Plebe Summer,* one— the Fourth Class Regiment); the First Regiment consists of Companies 1–18; the Second Regiment consists of Companies 19–36.

Registration (or Pre-Registration)—the practice, beginning with pre-registration about one-third of the way through an existing semester, of scheduling one's courses for the next semester; near the end of the existing semester, during registration, midshipmen may attempt to select their next-semester schedule from NADN; among those things considered in drawing up schedules: required courses, requested classes and teachers, availability, and *priority.*

Reg PE Gear—essentially mesh blue shorts, *blue-rim* T-shirt, and issue tube socks; winter issue are gray sweatshirt and sweatpants.

Regs—short for regulations, from Midshipman Regulations (MidRegs—now *CSORM*) ("What do the Regs say?" and "Look it up in the Regs").

Reorganization Week—a week at the end of *Plebe Summer* when Plebes are reorganized from their summer platoons into their academic-year Companies; also called "Admin Week."

Resign—(verb) to disenroll from the Academy; see *separation.*

Responses—the five biggies, the basic responses for Plebes: (1) "Yes, sir (or ma'am)"; (2) "No, sir"; (3) "No excuse, sir"; (4) "I'll find out, sir"; and (5) "Aye aye, sir."

Restriction—the serving of time for an infraction within the administrative conduct system; it consists primarily of (1) personnel *musters* in Smoke Hall at least twice a day for uniform inspections, and (2) confinement to one's Company area unless signed out for classes, the library, or athletics; a midshipman on restriction may not go outside The Yard; restriction is served by midshipmen over leave periods and may delay graduation if some restriction time remains; see *tour.*

Retention—the opposite of *separation;* a midshipman not "separated" is "retained."

Return of the Brigade—the night at the end of *Plebe Summer* when *upperclassmen* return from *summer training,* and Second Classmen formally introduce themselves to Plebes; dreaded by Plebes; now discouraged; see *Black Monday (or Sunday).*

Reveille—at 6:30 A.M., proclaimed by the ringing of the *bell* and announced from the Main Office over *1-MC* (by an upperclassman saying, "Reveille, reveille. All hands heave out and trice up. Man the hatches with overheads lighted. Now reveille."); midshipmen are supposed to get out of bed; the day's first obligation is 7:00 A.M. *officer's call* and *morning quarters* formation, which is followed by breakfast.

Reverse Halo Effect—see *halo effect.*

RHIP (RHIR)—acronym for Rank Has Its Privileges (Responsibilities): an expression of joy (or resignation).

Rig—(verb) to fit a uniform with its insignia, nametag, and devices.

Rig It!—formerly a command to a Plebe to elevate one's elbows and put one's turned-up hands on one's chin to hold it in; now a violation of Plebe Indoc (see *Indoc*), hence illegal.

Ring Dance—since 1925, the formal dance at the end of Second Class year (four days before graduation), at which Second Classmen are officially permitted to wear their *class rings.*

Ring Knocker—a midshipman or Academy graduate, especially one wearing a *class ring;* one who uses a ring to tap on tables in King Hall, on desks in classes, and on Plebes' doors; mildly derogatory.

Road Trip—ordinarily to any nearby college, ordinarily to seek and find the opposite sex.

Robomate—a computer terminal near each mate's (*CMOD's*) desk, used for Company purposes.

Rock—(noun) a midshipman who has extreme difficulty passing tests, such as those in academics ("ac rock"), professional knowledge ("pro rock"), and swimming ("aqua rock"); (verb) to be *slammed* ("My double-e prof really rocked me on the test grade").

The Rocks—large rip-rap on the Spa Creek seawall, often run on an *outer.*

Roger—a Navy-wide response meaning (1) "I have received and acknowledge your transmission," and (2) "yes" or *affirmative;* generically, often used with "that," as in: "Are you taking a weekend?" "Roger that."

Room Formal—see *inspections.*

Rooming—generally doubles and triples, with a few large rooms—called *barns*—containing four (more or less); there are few singles; the genders are not mixed within rooms, but men's rooms and women's rooms are interspersed throughout Bancroft—meaning that a room containing (for instance) two men will be situated next to a room containing two women; midshipmen may room only with members of the same Company and class; rooms are ordinarily selected in the spring—by class, with rising Firsties choosing first; see *scramble.*

Room Tour—an alternative to an area tour (see *tour*); a way to serve a tour without marching—because of exams, bad weather, or a cool *BOOW,* etc.

Rumble—a dated term for a more physical form of a *take out*—always Plebes vs. upperclassmen; illegal.

Rumor Triple-Star—from an NADN program code, a phrase meaning "through the grapevine"; e.g., "I heard it on Rumor Triple-Star."

Running-mate—an enlisted sailor or a junior officer assigned to a midshipman for, respectively, Second Class and First Class cruises during *summer training*.

Run Out—(verb) regarding a midshipman: to do everything he or she can to force or drive another out of the Academy; illegal.

Salty Sam—an annually replaced anonymous columnist in *The Log*, who dishes dirt and sarcastically questions the behavior of midshipmen and the administration.

Saluting—midshipmen salute all officers of the U.S. armed forces, plus officers of the Merchant Marine and the Public Health Service; those in the Navy and Marines salute with the right hand, but—contrary to those in the Army and Air Force—they may salute with the left if the right is encumbered; by custom, midshipmen sometimes salute midshipmen acquaintances with dates on The Yard; male midshipmen do not salute when their *covers* (hats) are off, which means they do not salute when inside or when seated (unless in a vehicle); female midshipmen do not remove their covers when inside, and do not salute there either; the rule for midshipmen is, salute when in doubt.

Sandblower—slang for a short individual; sometimes, a midshipman marching in the back of his or her Company during parades.

Sat—short for satisfactory: (1) one's academic average (see *CQPR, unsat,* and *gravy*); (2) acceptable in terms of military appearance or behavior.

Satellite Dish—a 12-meter parabolic antenna on Hospital Point: for the acquisition of "accurate weather information," satellite signals, and foreign-language broadcasts.

SATO—short for SATO Travel, the travel agency for the Brigade (and for families of midshipmen); in the basement of Bancroft's fifth wing.

Scramble—(verb) to change, or mix, Companies—a practice that varies; current practice is to "shotgun," or mix, all rising Youngsters into new Companies, no longer with their Plebe Company mates; another practice is to pair all Youngsters of one Company with those of another Company in another Regiment (for example, all the Youngsters in the 3rd Company might go to the 22nd, and vice-versa), and to scramble them at the end of their Third Class year, so that they spend their Second and First Class years in another Company; the administration decides annually on the method for that year's scramble; see *rooming.*

Screen—a midshipman (usually a Plebe) with mega *reverse halo effect;* a scapegoat; one who draws unusual attention to him or herself and catches a lot of flak, often resulting in punishment; short for a longer (offensive) phrase.

Screw the Pooch—(verb) to do poorly ("I really screwed the pooch on that double-e test").

Scrounge—(verb) to look hard for, as in a midshipman scrounging in King Hall for extra slices of cheese to *snake.*

SCUM—a mythical Academy group, the Society of Currently Unsat Midshipmen.

Scuttlebutt—(1) any drinking fountain; (2) any rumor.

SDBs—Navy-wide acronym for Service Dress Blues, the standard midshipman uniform for evenings, weekends, and off-campus wear during winter months; see *uniforms.*

Seabag Inspection—an inspection of a midshipman's issue-gear, to make sure he or she has retained all of it; ordinarily assigned only if a midshipman is in trouble.

SEAL—acronym for Sea, Air, Land: the Navy's combination frog-man/paratrooper/commando used for insertion, extraction, counter-insurgency, and reconnaissance; hence, a Navy commando; see *BUD/S* and *Mini-BUD/S.*

Sea Lawyer—a midshipman, usually a Plebe, who excessively niggles or makes excuses.

Seawall—any reinforced water's edge on The Yard along the Severn River or along Spa or Dorsey Creeks.

Second Class—a member of the Second Class; the equivalent of a junior at a civilian college; see *Plebe, Youngster,* and *Firstie.*

Second Class Alley—in King Hall, any aisle between rows of tables where only members of the Second (or First) Class may walk when going to and from *tables;* see *First Class alley.*

Second Class Entry—either of two side entrances to Bancroft's third and fourth wings from Tecumseh Court; see *T-Court.*

Second Class Loan—the popular name for a career starter loan: any of various loans offered to midshipmen at the end of Second Class year by Navy Mutual Aid and several civilian banks, and frequently accepted for the purchase of (among other things) a car.

Section Leader—a midshipman designated by the instructor (or "volunteered" by his or her classmates) to take attendance in each class (not a glamorous job); for *academic accountability,* the instructor submits via computer a daily accountability report indicating those tardy and absent.

Segundo—an occasional nickname for a member of the Second Class.

Separation—the act of disenrolling from the Academy; voluntary resignation or involuntary discharge (or dismissal); midshipmen separating voluntarily after the beginning of Second Class year may have to pay considerable reimbursements—approaching $100,000—calculated by the Academy; in addition, those separating in their Second or First Class years must usually serve in the *fleet* as enlistees for up to two or three years, respectively; all separations are approved by the Secretary of the Navy; see *retention* and *sep pen.*

Sep Pen—short for Separation Pending, meaning a midshipman whose separation from the Academy is in limbo, awaiting administrative disposition: The midshipman may, or may not, depart the Academy; a midshipman not separated is "retained."

Service Assignment—the day (and night) shortly after the end of Christmas leave, when First Classmen are assigned their warfare specialty—the Navy or Marine community in which they will serve following graduation; see *PQ.*

Sets—(1) the two halves of *Plebe Summer,* called the First and Second Sets (upperclassmen in the *Plebe Detail* in charge of Plebe training are different in each set); (2) the two halves of the academic year, called the First and Second Sets, as they relate to *stripers.*

Severn River Hip Disease—a mythical malady of mysterious origin, the effects of which are sometimes attributed by certain midshipmen to the high caloric content of food served in King Hall.

Sheet Posters—prepared seemingly without end by Plebes for display inside and outside Bancroft to promote Brigade spirit.

Ships—nickname for an advanced (and required) course in *boats* taken by naval architects.

Ships and Aircraft—a reference book, issued to Plebes, containing voluminous fleet information.

Shotgun—to scatter a Plebe class at the end of Plebe year and put its members into other Companies; see *scramble.*

Shoulder Boards—shoulder designations of rank; also known as "boards."

Shove Off—(verb) (1) to leave, go away—often used in King Hall ("Shove off, scrounge"); (2) to be released from a required duty ("I got shoved off from a chow call").

Sick Call—one of three designated periods during the day when midshipmen may go to *Medical* with real or imagined afflictions.

The Silent Service—a Navy-wide term for the submarine community.

Single-E—slang for an English or economics major; see *Double-E.*

SIR (pronounced *ess-eye-are*)—acronym for Sick in Room (in the fleet, known as SIQ—Sick in Quarters).

Sir (Ma'am)—the appropriate form of address or response by any subordinate in conversation with a superior; Plebes enter dangerous water if they "*sss-ma'am*" or "sir, er ma'am" a female upperclass (or vice-versa).

Six-N—a dreaded day with six classes (the maximum) in a midshipman's academic schedule; also Five-N, Four-N, etc.

Skate—(noun) anything that is easy; (verb) to exert little effort ("I skated that class").

Skivvies—a Navy-wide term for underdrawers or briefs.

Skivvy Waver—a Navy-wide slang term for a signalman, an expert at communicating with flags.

Slack—reduced discipline; see *cut (me) some slack.*

Slam—(verb) (1) to nail or get nailed, as in doing particularly well ("I slammed that test") or being hit particularly hard, usually for an infraction ("He slammed me"); see *power slam.*

Sliders—see *Z burgers.*

Slime—(noun) (1) a disreputable individual or one possessing unflattering characteristics ("He turned me in, the slime"); also, "scum," as in "scumbag"; (2) poor performance ("That's slime, Plebe"); (verb) (1) to turn sloppy or mushy corners as a Plebe ("He was sliming through the Hall"); (2) to get a woman drunk and then take advantage of her ("He slimed her").

Smack—a brown-noser, an apple-polisher, a digger, a suck; also used as a verb.

Smile—(1) the curved indention in a properly rolled (and, when the curve is up, properly shelved) pair of socks; (2) the shape formed when the black elastic on a *cover* slips too low ("Fix your cover's smile").

Smoke—(verb) to do well (transitive) ("I smoked that test") or poorly (intransitive) ("I got smoked by that test").

Snake—(verb) to take anybody else's anything, notably the date of another midshipman; also used as a noun—i.e., one who takes something.

Snake-Eater—a nickname for members of both the *SEALs* and Marine Recon.

Snarf—(verb) (1) to swipe or steal; (2) to eat quickly by large bites ("He snarfed down four pancakes in two minutes").

Snipe—one serving in a ship's engineering department.

SOP (pronounced *ess-oh-pee*)—military-wide abbreviation for Standard Operating Procedure ("It's SOP; it's the way they do things around here").

Sound Off—(verb) to shout or yell; what Plebes do when they square corners in Bancroft: shout a motivational phrase (such as "Beat Army!"), and follow it by "Sir!" or "Ma'am!"; also, what members of the Brigade staff do during formal parades; see *plates* and *square corners.*

Spawning Ground of the Navy—the Naval Academy.

Splashdown—any dance, usually an impromptu one in a Bancroft hallway or basement.

Sponge—(1) a midshipman who easily soaks up knowledge; (2) a chronic borrower; (3) something that draws fire.

Sponsors—the Academy's closest approximation of *in loco parentis*—hundreds of Annapolis-area residents, many with Academy ties, who open their houses to midshipmen; every midshipman has a designated sponsor to whose house he or she may go when on liberty to hang out, let his or her hair down, or do whatever; sponsors frequently become counselors and confidants and friends—and are particularly helpful during Plebe Year; they are magnanimous and underpaid (they receive no stipend); in late fall, the Academy sometimes honors them with a weekend that includes special recognition and a dinner in King Hall.

Spook—a nickname for a spy or a member of the intelligence community; see *Intel.*

Spoon—(verb) regarding an upperclassman: officially to tell a Plebe the upperclassman's name ("I'm spooning you: Call me Arnie"); regarding a Plebe: to have that event happen ("Mr. Jones spooned me today: He said to call him Arnie"); frequently occurs among midshipmen on athletic teams; discouraged by the administration because it implies a breakdown of the official Plebe Indoctrination System, especially if it occurs too early in Plebe year; see *Indoc.*

SPUDS—a nickname for *BUD/S.*

Squad—the smallest unit of organization within the Brigade, generally consisting of about a dozen midshipmen; there are three Squads per Platoon and nine Squads per Company.

Squad Leader—a Firstie; a one-striper billet, changed every semester.

Squad Tables—see *tables.*

Square Corners—(verb) to perform the Plebe rite of making all turns in Bancroft hallways at 90 degrees while saying, "Go Navy, sir! Beat Army, sir!" (or "ma'am!"); an upperclassman might say, "Plebe, square those corners!"; see *plates* and *sound off.*

Squid—a nickname for midshipmen, employed almost exclusively by cadets at the Air Force Academy and West Point; Naval Academy reciprocals for them are (Air Force) "Zoomies" or "Bus Drivers" and (West Point) "Kaydets" or "Woops"—the last said to be (1) from the noise of the flying monkeys in "The Wizard of Oz" (the monkeys wore capes similar to the capes integral to the West Point uniform), and (2) from the earlier term Woo-Poos, formed from the *W* and *P* in West Point.

Squid Bait—see *mid hawk.*

SQPR *(s-kyooper)*—acronym for Semester Quality Point Ratio (see *Order of Merit* and *CQPR*).

Star—(verb) to make the *Superintendent's List,* and thus to win the right to wear a gold star (a "supe star") on certain uniforms; also, sometimes, to make the *Dean's List* and thus to win the right to wear a bronze star.

Station—a Navy-wide term for any place where one serves duty; see *duty station.*

Steam—a required engineering course, generally *Thermo* for non–Group I majors.

St. John's—a collegiate *croquet* power down the street.

Steerage—a restaurant for all midshipmen (nights only); in Bancroft, between third and fourth wings, adjacent to Smoke Hall; see *Drydock* and *Galley.*

Stoked—really pumped, excited, or prepared ("I'm stoked for the game").

Storage—generally, the mandatory storing of personal items, including computers, in the basement during summer vacation.

Strak—excessively by the book, overly strict—particularly in performance and military demands.

Striper—a midshipman officer: (1) a First Classman with rank in the Company or in the Brigade, so designated by the stripes of braid on his or her shoulder boards and sleeves; usually a three striper or above; a mega (or super) striper is one with four, five, or six stripes; the stripes have name equivalents to rank in the *fleet;* in both *sets* only rarely will a Firstie besides a Brigade Commander (notably captains in sailing and crew) wear a total exceeding six stripes (e.g., if two in the first *set* then no more than four in the second); (2) a non-Firstie striper, usually a Second Class assisting a Firstie in the striper organizational network.

Striper Billet—the position designated or held in a *striper* chain of command.

Striper Dick (or Striper Dork)—a *striper* whose position has gone to his or her head; one who uses his or her power to an excessive degree; a *tool.*

Striper Ranking—of midshipmen in a Company.

Sub Squad—a special-regime group for those having trouble with swimming tests; midshipmen tend to call all squads for those judged *PE deficient* "sub squads"; see *conditioning squad* and *PE deficient.*

Suck It Up—(verb) to accept a situation, to buckle down and deal with it ("With four tests and two papers next week, you'll just have to suck it up" or "You got a 5,000 for going over the wall, so suck it up"); "take the strain."

Summer Elective Training—options include scuba, sloop cruises, jump school (airborne) at Ft. Benning, mini-BUD/S at Coronado, SERE (Survival, Evasion, Resistance, and Escape), the Pentagon, foreign exchange, foreign language training abroad, and research projects; see *summer training.*

Summer School—some courses are taught at the Academy during the summer for makeup and enrichment.

Summer Training—following *Commissioning Week* (and sometimes prior to it), all midshipmen in the three remaining classes have leave or some form of professional training—generally for eight weeks; see *blocks* and *summer elective training.*

Summer Whites—see *uniforms.*

Supe—short for the *Superintendent;* often when the Superintendent is present, midshipmen will chant, "Supe! Supe!"

Supe's List—short for *Superintendent's List.*

Superintendent—No. 1; the highest-ranking official at the Naval Academy.

Superintendent's List—a midshipman makes the list in any semester with (1) a semester QPR of at least 3.4, (2) no grades below a C in the semester, (3) an A in *performance,* (4) an A in *conduct,* and (5) at least a B in physical education—an achievement generally attained by fewer than about 6 percent of the Brigade; see *Dean's List* and *Commandant's List.*

Surface Nuke—see *nuke.*

Swarrior—a nickname for a surface-warfare officer (see *SWO*).

Sweat—a midshipman who worries about everything ("He's a sweat"); also a verb meaning to worry excessively ("Don't sweat it").

Sweat Box—any area in Bancroft where midshipmen do *PT.*

Sweet—a widely used expression meaning great, cool, terrific, *high speed,* etc.

SWO—(1) a surface-warfare officer; (2) the surface-warfare option—i.e., the surface Navy ("I'm going SWO"); the "O" is long, as in "hope"; see *SWOS.*

SWO-Daddy—a nickname for a surface-warfare officer; also a surface officer who takes a younger officer under his or her wing; see *SWO.*

SWOS—acronym for Surface Warfare Officer School; the "O" is short, as in "Oscar."

SWO Sweater—a midshipman's sweater, identical to those worn in the fleet.

Tables—short for squad tables, the regular arrangement for dining in King Hall; frequently used in the phrase "at tables" ("We were at tables, and he dropped the tray" or "Are you going down to tables?"); see *team tables* and *hot seat.*

Tac—military jargon for a hyphen, as in *1-90.*

TACAMO—acronym for Take Charge and Move Out.

TAD (pronounced *tee-a-dee*)—acronym for Temporary Additional Duty: at the Academy, the duty served between Commissioning and an Academy graduate's first *duty station;* the duty is "temporary" because it normally lasts less than six months; duty longer than six months (and usually involving a move) is ordinarily defined as a permanent change of station (PCS).

Tailgating—a post-event parent/guardian/sponsor tradition at certain sports contests—notably football, lacrosse, and crew.

Take a Strain for Navy—do it; suck it up; exert yourself; sweat for Navy ("C'mon! Five more push-ups! Take a strain!").

Take Out—(verb) regarding Plebes: to "get" an upperclassman, usually in some organized fashion; to harass an upperclassman mildly—for example with shaving cream, and often during fests in a shower or bathroom; taking out an upperclassman violates *1-90* and is highly discouraged by the administration; see *rumble.*

Tango Company—during Plebe Summer, for those who want to leave the Academy.

Taps—"when you have to be back"; the time when midshipmen must be in their Company area for an *accountability* muster: for Plebes, 11 P.M., except Saturday; for upperclassmen, midnight, except Saturday; for all midshipmen, Saturday taps is 1:00 A.M. Sunday.

TBS—acronym for *The Basic School* in Quantico, Virginia.

T-Court—short for Tecumseh Court, in front of Bancroft; it takes its name from the nearby bronze statue called *Tecumseh,* at which some midshipmen toss pennies for good luck on exams.

Teacher Evals—forms, filled out at the end of each semester prior to final exams, on which midshipmen write their opinions of their teachers and courses; midshipmen have the option of signing their names or submitting the forms anonymously; a given form is read by both the teacher and by his or her department chairman; also called "Get Back Sheets" and "Slam Sheets."

Team 6,000 (or 5,500, or 5,000, or whatever)—a motivational phrase comprising all the midshipmen and Naval Academy staff.

Team Tables—as opposed to squad tables (see *tables*): meal tables for in-season varsity athletes—designed to promote team unity in a non-athletic environment, and to accommodate irregular practice times ("We've got late tables tonight"); no special food is served.

Tecumseh—actually (at the Academy) a bronze statue of Tamanend, a peaceful Delaware chief (the sachem from whom New York's Tammany Hall takes its name)—long ago nicknamed by midshipmen "Tecumseh," after the war-loving Shawnee chief; frequently called the "god of 2.0" (see *unsat*); some midshipmen toss pennies at Tecumseh en route to their exams for good luck, trying to get the pennies in his quiver; see *T-Court*.

Telephone—the main link with the outside; calls in, via messages through the Main Office, are easily do-able—and the messages are usually delivered (and delivery is aided if you know the midshipman's room number); messages also are delivered by e-mail; midshipmen cannot be called directly; in nearly all cases, midshipmen at the Academy have to call you.

10-Meter Board—the diving platform, close to the ceiling of Lejeune Hall, from which all Youngsters must jump as part of a swim test (midshipmen must jump from this or one of the two lower boards once in each of their three other years); failure to jump may lead to a midshipman's being denied graduation; also called "the tower."

Thanksgiving Rule—a mythical dictum holding that a Plebe with a steady prior to induction will break up by Thanksgiving; see *2% Club*.

Thermo—short for courses in thermodynamics.

Three Chews and a Swallow—a motivational technique formerly practiced during *Plebe Summer* in connection with Plebe training; an added purpose was to "encourage" Plebes to take small bites of their food in command situations; now contrary to Plebe Indoctrination (see *Indoc*).

Tool—a jerk.

Tour—(1) disciplinary punishment for a military infraction, wherein the guilty party erases demerits by marching 45-minute segments on weekends or holidays in an area so designated for each Battalion, either outside or inside (usually near the Battalion office); all classes serve tours, though tours are generally given for lesser infractions, and (contrary to those on restriction) midshipmen given tours may go on liberty once they have marched or served their tours; in-season athletes may have their tours deferred until season's end; see *EMI;* (2) a Navy-wide term for a *billet* or *duty station:* those in the Navy will usually alternate between sea tours and shore tours; those in the Marines will usually alternate between staff (or desk) tours and foreign or domestic combat-training tours.

Tower—see *10-meter board.*

Townie—one who dwells in *Crabtown.*

Town Liberty—liberty within the vicinity of Annapolis and the Naval Academy; generally (1) for Firsties, every day except Wednesday until *taps;* (2) for Second Class, Friday, Saturday, and Sunday, and Tuesday if they have a B in both conduct and performance and are not academically or PE deficient; (3) for Youngsters, Saturday and Sunday, and Friday if they have a B in both conduct and performance and are not academically or PE deficient; (4) for Plebes, Saturday; see *liberty, yard liberty,* and *leave.*

The Trident—a weekly tabloid newspaper produced by the Academy's Public Affairs Office; it appears on Fridays 49 times per year and is available by subscription.

Trident Scholar—one of a few brainy and/or well-rounded Firsties authorized to take a reduced class load in order to complete a major research project.

. . . Triple Star—any of numerous Academy computer programs, accessed by adding a preliminary word or phrase, for use by midshipmen and Academy staff.

Triton Light—a monument at the corner of The Yard where the Severn River and Spa Creek seawalls join.

Trucker's English—slang for a lower-level course in English grammar for a small number of Plebes and Youngsters.

Tuck—(noun) a fold in the back of a uniform's shirt to give it a neat appearance; (verb) to make such a fold or crease. Plebes are expected to be connoisseurs of the tuck, often requiring the assistance of a classmate standing behind to meet the standard ("My roommate gave me a tuck"); "shirt stays" help retain the tuck, and many upperclass require Plebes to wear them.

Turf Field—see *The Driveway.*

2 for 8—the point of no return, passed when Second Classmen enter their first academic class in their Second Class year; at about the same time, Second Class also sign, before a witness, a commitment to service, which spells out what happens if they leave the Academy (including costs, possibly in the $100,000 range, they must repay the Academy); thereby, they agree to two more years at the Academy plus generally a six-year service obligation following graduation; 2 for 8 is celebrated by a huge class tailgate during football season.

Two-Inch Bulk Rule—the Navy regulation that for female midshipmen the volume (or mass) of the *hair* may not extend up or out more than two inches from the head.

2% Club—a mythical group whose members are those midshipmen—purportedly 2% of those with steady dating relationships begun prior to induction—whose relationships survive until graduation; see *Thanksgiving Rule.*

2.0 and Go—a phrase referring to the grade point average necessary for graduation.

UA—abbreviation for Unauthorized Absence; it used to be the broader military term AWOL (for Absent Without Leave).

Uncover—(verb) to remove one's midshipman's *cover* (or any hat) when going inside.

Underclass (or Underclassman)—interchangeable terms for any midshipman except a Firstie; not used as frequently as *upperclass* (or *upperclassman*).

Uniforms—during the academic day, midshipmen wear their working uniforms—summer blues (short-sleeved) in warm and hot weather or winter blues (long-sleeved) in cool and cold; outside

The Yard, they wear summer whites or service dress blues (SDBs), depending on the season; numerous other uniforms exist for special and/or dressy occasions—among them: khakis, full dress whites (choker whites), and full dress blues (chokers, or FDBs).

Uniform Races—Plebe Summer practices designed (1) to promote familiarity with the Navy uniform, and (2) to teach speed in getting in and out of it; see *rack races*.

Un-reg—any action, behavior, procedure, condition, or attire contrary to regulations; sometimes "non-reg."

Unsat—(1) short for unsatisfactory in terms of dress or behavior ("That's unsat, Mister"); (2) the condition of (a) having an academic average below 2.0, or (b) having an F or two Ds at the end of a grading period; see *academically deficient, Order of Merit,* and *sat.*

Upperclass (or Upperclassman)—interchangeable terms for any midshipman except a Plebe ("He's an upperclass" or "She's an upperclassman"); see *underclass* (or *underclassman*).

Use the Force—from Obi-wan's advice to Luke Skywalker in the movie *Star Wars:* a phrase employed to urge a friend not to date another midshipman ("Use the Force; resist the Dark Side"); see *Ben "Obi-Wan" Kenobi.*

Using My Honor Against Me—a midshipman feeling he or she is in a situation in which information is being wrongly demanded, might say that to divulge the information "would be using my honor against me"; a midshipman might use the phrase when he or she feels certain questions about conduct are unfounded or unwarranted (for example, "Did you break any rules this weekend?"); the Academy's approximation of the Constitution's Fifth Amendment defense against self-incrimination.

Validate—generally, to test out of: (1) to get academic credit for, particularly as a Plebe; (2) to perform outstandingly on a PE test before the scheduled beginning of that PE segment (see *pre-test*).

VGEP—acronym for Volunteer Graduate Education Program, a competitive program open to midshipmen highly proficient in academics; under VGEP, in their second semester First Classmen may take courses toward master's degrees at any of seven nearby colleges—

generally with completion of the degree program by the end of the calendar year in which they graduate from the Academy.

Videos—commercial studios make available to parents a wide variety of videos about various aspects of Academy life (*I-Day, Plebe Summer, Herndon, Commissioning Week,* the full academic year, etc.); in some cases arrangements can be made to include footage of a specific midshipman; the studios advertise the videos by mail.

Visitor Center—where tourists go; few midshipmen do.

Walk-Through—see *inspections.*

The Wall—the structure separating The Yard from the rest of Annapolis—The Yard's boundary on two sides; midshipmen occasionally "jump the wall"—i.e., breach the wall's integrity; see *Gate Zero* and *over the wall.*

Wall of Shame—a posted list of those who quit during Plebe Summer.

Wanna-Be—someone who wants too desperately to become something, and frequently acts that way ("He's a Marine wanna-be").

Wardroom—short for *Company wardroom.*

Warfare Designation Pin—see *blood pins.*

Warfare Specialty Schools—*SWOS, BUD/S, The Basic School, Navy Flight School,* Nuclear Power School *(NPS),* etc., for training of officers after commissioning.

Watch—a duty of all midshipmen and most Navy personnel; an obligation in Bancroft consisting of rotating watch duties, some of which—through the years—are *CDO, CMOD, MOM, BOM, OOW, CMOW,* and *BOOW.*

Water Wings—slang for the Surface Warfare breast insignia.

Weekend Eligible—midshipmen may not be eligible to take weekends (that is, they may be non-weekend eligible) (1) if they have a QPR below 2.15 or if they have two Ds or one F (see *academically deficient*), (2) if they are on *restriction,* (3) if they are on any kind of *probation,* or (4) if they have any deficiency or are on any *sub squad.*

West Point—in Highland Falls, New York: its class designations—in order—are Plebe, Yearling, Cow, Firstie; see *classes* and *Air Force Academy.*

Whatever Flips Your Skirt—a phrase said in response to a statement about any preference ("You like triple-dip ice-cream cones? You like to study in church? Whatever flips your skirt"); also, "whatever floats your boat."

Whiskey Lima—see *WL.*

Whiskey Tango—see *WT.*

Whites—short for Summer Whites; see *uniforms.*

Wingman—from the aviation term: one's constant companion, strongest supporter, or closest confidant ("My roommates are great, but so-and-so is my wingman"); also, "wingie."

Wings—(1) pilot's wings, jump wings, etc.; (2) the eight primary sections of Bancroft Hall; each consists of five floors (or decks) for living, plus two basement levels (the seventh and eighth wings have a mezzanine level between their basements and their first floors); numbering of the living floors is 0–4; midshipmen discussing where they live will commonly cite their wing and their floor, in that order—e.g., (a) a midshipman living on 5-0 resides in the fifth wing on the zero deck (the first residential floor), and (b) a midshipman living on 6-2 resides in the sixth wing on the second deck (the third residential floor); (3) a slang term for the women's uniform necktie.

Wires—the level of electrical engineering taken by non-engineering majors; see *cables.*

WL—from the phonetic alphabet, Whiskey Lima: a male midshipman who pursues female midshipmen.

Woop—see *squid.*

Wreck—(verb) (1) to consume too much alcohol ("He got wrecked"); (2) to be done in by someone or something ("The test wrecked me").

WRNV—the midshipman-run FM radio station, complete with midshipmen disc jockeys; located in the basement of Bancroft's eighth wing (by contrast, WNAV is an AM commercial station in Annapolis).

WT—from the phonetic alphabet, Whiskey Tango: synonym for a *bag it;* also, someone undependable, a weak link in the human chain.

W.T. Door—Joe Doakes, Midshipman Anybody: a term in diminishing usage describing the typical midshipman; he rooms with Joe Gish; the two live next to the Company Officer.

WUBA (pronounced *woo-ba*)—acronym for Working Uniform Blue Alpha, the former name for midshipmen's winter working uniform (now called Winter Working Blues, *WWBs*); formerly a derogatory name used for women midshipmen; see *WL.*

WWBs—acronym for Winter Working Blues, the standard midshipman class-day uniform during winter months; see *uniforms.*

X-Period—during X-Weeks, a period prior to first period to facilitate the scheduling and taking of tests.

X-Week—any week in which a series of exams occurs; usually the week prior to the issuance of six- and twelve-week grades.

The Yard—the Academy campus.

Yard Engine—a rarely used term for a datable girl who lives on The Yard.

Yard Liberty—liberty anywhere on, but restricted to, The Yard; all midshipmen have it from 5:30 A.M. until *taps;* see *liberty, town liberty,* and *leave.*

Yard Mail—non-postal mail among Academy buildings; similar to a civilian company's inter-office mail.

Youngster—(1) a member of the Third Class; the equivalent of a sophomore at a civilian college; see *Plebe, Second Class,* and *Firstie;* (2) sleep time: a day (or "Youngster Afternoon") when a midshipman has no classes after lunch (i.e., during fifth and sixth periods); see *civilian.*

Youngster Bridge(s)—the low walls along the sidewalks on either side of Chauvenet and Michelson, supposedly not for use by Plebes.

Youngster Cruise—part of required *summer training* for rising Youngsters, consisting of about a month on either (1) one of the Academy's Yard Patrol (*YP*) craft, or (2) one of the Navy's 44-foot sloops (with emphasis on navigation and seamanship); the other part of the summer consists of four weeks of Marine Corps leadership training in Quantico, Virginia (including land navigation, weapons indoctrination, and small-unit tactics); see *First Class cruise* and *summer training.*

Youngster Ladder—any Bancroft stairway narrow enough that one's extended arms can touch both walls; not for use by Plebes.

Youngster Summer—see *Youngster cruise.*

You're Down!—a phrase meaning "You're in trouble," the especially deep variety.

YP—any of several 108-foot-long Yard Patrol craft stationed at the Academy; often used in conjunction with professional, leadership, and navigational courses—as well as for *summer training.*

Z Burgers—Academy hamburgers, so named for their alleged power to induce sleep (Zs) in those who eat them—particularly in those who eat them at lunch and then go to fifth- or sixth-period class (during the *Dark Ages,* the combination of Z burgers and a Youngster afternoon [see *Youngster*] is coveted and revered); also called "sliders."

Zebra Effect—the scene in *T-Court* when the word about uniform change in spring and fall has not gotten fully around, and some uniforms are at the cleaners or in the laundry, and some midshipmen show up for *formation* in the old uniform when the new one is called for.

Zenith—the personal computer issued to every midshipman at the end of Plebe Summer; purchased by monthly requisitions from pay; mandated for retention until graduation.

Zero Dark Thirty—early; when too many midshipmen awaken each morning, primarily in the winter; also "Oh Dark Thirty."

Zoomie—see *squid.*

APPENDIX

"ANCHOR'S AWEIGH"

(Words by Midshipman Alfred Hart Miles [1906]; music by the Academy's bandmaster and choir director, Lieutenant Charles Zimmermann; first played publicly at the Army-Navy game in November, 1906.)

> *Anchor's aweigh, my boys,*
> *Anchor's aweigh,*
> *Farewell to college joys*
> *We sail at break of day,*
> *Through our last night on shore,*
> *Drink to the foam.*
> *Until we meet once more,*
> *Here's wishing you a happy voyage home.*

And:

> *Stand Navy down the field,*
> *Sails set to the sky,*

We'll never change our course,
So Army you steer shy.
Roll up the score, Navy,
Anchor's aweigh,
Sail Navy down the field
And sink the Army, sink the Army Grey.

CODE OF CONDUCT

(Issued April 17, 1955, by President Dwight Eisenhower, with slight modifications since then; intended to codify the principles by which members of the military should live, notably when held prisoner. This is the current version.)

I. I am an American. I serve in the forces which guard my country and our way of life. I am prepared to give my life in their defense.

II. I will never surrender of my own free will. If in command I will never surrender the members of my command while they still have the means to resist.

III. If I am captured I will continue to resist by all means available. I will make every effort to escape and aid others to escape. I will accept neither parole nor special favors from the enemy.

IV. If I become a prisoner of war, I will keep faith with my fellow prisoners. I will give no information or take part in any action which might be harmful to my comrades. If I am senior, I will take command. If not, I will obey the lawful orders of those appointed over me and will back them up in every way.

V. When questioned, should I become a prisoner of war, I am required to give name, rank, service number, and date of birth. I will evade answering further questions to the utmost of my ability. I will make no oral or written statements disloyal to my country and its allies or harmful to their cause.

VI. I will never forget that I am an American, responsible for my actions and dedicated to the principles which made my country free. I will trust in my God and in the United States of America.

HONOR CONCEPT

Midshipmen are persons of integrity: They stand for that which is right.

A. They tell the truth and ensure that the full truth is known. They do not lie.

B. They embrace fairness in all actions. They ensure that work submitted as their own is their own, and that assistance received from any source is authorized and properly documented. They do not cheat.

C. They respect the property of others and ensure that others are able to benefit from the use of their own property. They do not steal.

"THE MARINES' HYMN"

(First published in 1918; music similar to "Couplets des Deux Hommes d'Armes" from Jacques Offenbach's 1868 comic operetta *Genevieve de Brabant;* the words have been attributed to various Marines—including Henry Davis, L. Z. Phillips, and Charles Doyen; in 1929 the Marine Corps adopted the three following verses as the official version.)

> *From the Halls of Montezuma*
> *To the shores of Tripoli;*
> *We fight our country's battles*
> *In the air, on land, and sea;*
> *First to fight for right and freedom*
> *And to keep our honor clean;*
> *We are proud to claim the title*
> *Of United States Marine.*

Our flag's unfurled to every breeze
  From dawn to setting sun;
We have fought in ev'ry clime and place
  Where we could take a gun;
In the snow of far off northern lands
  And in sunny tropic scenes;
You will find us always on the job—
  The United States Marines.

Here's health to you and to our Corps
  Which we are proud to serve
In many a strife we've fought for life
  And never lost our nerve;
If the Army and the Navy
  Ever look on Heaven's scenes
They will find the streets are guarded
  By United States Marines.

THE PRAYER OF A MIDSHIPMAN

(Written by Chaplain William Thomas; first read at the "Sob Sunday" graduation service in the Chapel in June, 1938.)

Almighty father, whose way is in the sea, whose paths are in the great waters, whose command is over all and whose love never faileth: Let me be aware of Thy presence and obedient to Thy will. Keep me true to my best self, guarding me against dishonesty in purpose and in deed, and helping me so to live that I can stand unashamed and unafraid before my shipmates, my loved ones, and Thee. Protect those in whose love I live. Give me the will to do my best and to accept my share of responsibilities with a strong heart and a cheerful mind. Make me considerate of those entrusted to my leadership and faithful to the duties my country has entrusted in me. Let my uniform remind me daily of the traditions of the service of which I am a part. If I am inclined to doubt, steady my faith; if I am tempted, make me strong to resist; if I should miss the mark, give me the courage to try again. Guide me with the light of truth and give me strength to faithfully serve Thee, now and always. Amen.

MISSION OF THE UNITED STATES NAVAL ACADEMY

To develop midshipmen morally, mentally, and physically and to imbue them with the highest ideals of duty, honor, and loyalty in order to provide graduates who are dedicated to a career of naval service and have potential for future development in mind and character to assume the highest responsibilities of command, citizenship, and government.

"NAVY BLUE AND GOLD" (NAVAL ACADEMY ALMA MATER)

(Words by Lieutenant Roy de Saussure Horn, [USNA, 1915]; music by Chapel choirmaster and organist Professor Joseph Crosley. First sung in the spring of 1923 at a Glee Club concert. Adopted as the Academy anthem in 1925.)

> *Now college men from sea to sea*
> *May sing of colors true,*
> *But who has better right than we*
> *To hoist a symbol hue?*
> *For sailor men in battle fair*
> *Since fighting days of old,*
> *Have proved the sailor's right to wear*
> *The Navy Blue and Gold.*

"NAVY HYMN"

(Words by William Whiting, 1860; music by John B. Dykes, 1861.)

> *Eternal Father, strong to save,*
> *Whose arm hath bound the restless wave,*
> *Who bidst the mighty ocean deep*
> *Its own appointed limits keep;*
> *Oh, hear us when we cry to thee*
> *For those in peril on the sea!*
> *Amen.*

OATH OF OFFICE FOR MIDSHIPMAN CANDIDATES

I, ———, having been appointed a midshipman in the United States Navy, do solemnly swear (or affirm) that I will support and defend the Constitution of the United States against all enemies, foreign and domestic; that I will bear true faith and allegiance to the same; that I take this obligation freely, without any mental reservation or purpose of evasion; and that I will well and faithfully discharge the duties of the office on which I am about to enter, So Help Me God.

[The foregoing is similar to the oath taken by midshipmen at their commissioning as Navy ensigns or Marine Corps second lieutenants.]

SEAL

(Designed by Park Benjamin [USNA 1867] and adopted by the Navy Department as the Academy's seal on January 25, 1899.)

The Naval Academy seal has for its crest Neptune's hand holding his trident aloft. Below the trident is a shield depicting an ancient galley coming bows-on into action; under the galley is an open book, indicative of education. Torches flank the shield. Beneath all is the motto "Ex Scientia Tridens" (From Knowledge, Sea Power).

PHOTO CAPTIONS

Frontispiece: The Chapel, also called the Cathedral of the Navy.

Page viii: The midshipman's shoulder boards (Plebes, no stripes; Youngsters, one diagonal stripe; Second Class, two diagonal stripes; First Class, one horizontal stripe).

Page ix: The United States Naval Academy from the air. The view looks southwest, with (from the bottom) Spa Creek, Farragut Field, Bancroft Hall, and the Chapel (center). Halsey Field House is to the left and Santee Basin and the Sailing Center to the right.

Page 2: A member of the Plebe detail (here a Firstie) addresses her Plebes during Plebe Summer.

Page 3: Induction Day, or I-day; in early July, a new class of Plebes is sworn in.

Page 10: Noon meal formation in Tecumseh Court, as viewed from the statue of Tamanend—called Tecumseh by the midshipmen. Beyond is the entrance to Bancroft Hall.

Page 11: The bronze statue of Tamanend, a Delaware chief, stands opposite the main entrance to Bancroft Hall. Long ago nicknamed Tecumseh by the midshipmen, the statue gives its name to Tecumseh Court, which it overlooks.

Page 30: An upperclassman in a physics lab.

Page 31: King Hall—as viewed from its central point, called the Anchor—is the Academy's wardroom, or dining hall. Located in Bancroft, it feeds the Brigade of Midshipmen in 20 minutes. It is shaped in the form of a T.

Page 41: Midshipmen standing in ranks on Worden field—the Academy's parade ground.

Page 58: Plebe Summer's Physical Education Program, or PEP, takes place early each morning on the synthetic-turf field.

Page 59: A midshipman on a summer training exercise.

Page 67: Alumni Hall, the Academy's newest major structure, was completed in 1991. It houses a 6,500-seat multipurpose arena and the Bob Hope Performing Arts Center with a 2,400-square-foot stage. Plebes begin their processing there on I-day.

Page 74: At Service Assignment. Following Christmas vacation, First Class midshipmen are assigned the warfare specialty in which they will spend their military careers.

Page 85: Herndon, a 21-foot obelisk near the Chapel. A Plebe removes a Plebe dixie-cup sailor's hat from the greased obelisk in late May, and the dixie cup's replacement by a midshipman's cover marks the symbolic end to Plebe Year.

Page 123: An 1853 etching of the Naval Academy, showing old Fort Severn (center).

Page 198: Newly commissioned midshipmen (Navy ensigns or Marine second lieutenants) toss their covers into the air, culminating their four-year career at the Academy.

Page 199: Midshipmen on parade.

Page 205: The Naval Academy seal.

INDEX

Note: Readers using this index should refer also to the specific alphabetical listings in the Glossary, pages 123–97.

Note: Readers using this index should refer also to the specific alphabetical listings in the Glossary, pages 123–97.

Note: Readers using this index should refer also to the specific alphabetical listings in the Glossary, pages 123–97.

Note: Readers using this index should refer also to the specific alphabetical listings in the Glossary, pages 123–97.

ABOUT THE AUTHOR

Ross Mackenzie is the father of two recent Naval Academy graduates. Runner-up for the Pulitzer Prize in commentary (1982), he has been a newspaper editor for 30 years in Richmond, Virginia, where he currently is Editor of the Editorial Pages of the *Richmond Times-Dispatch*.

THE NAVAL INSTITUTE PRESS is the book-publishing arm of the U.S. Naval Institute, a private, nonprofit, membership society for sea service professionals and others who share an interest in naval and maritime affairs. Established in 1873 at the U.S. Naval Academy in Annapolis, Maryland, where its offices remain today, the Naval Institute has members worldwide.

Members of the Naval Institute support the education programs of the society and receive the influential monthly magazine *Proceedings* and discounts on fine nautical prints and on ship and aircraft photos. They also have access to the transcripts of the Institute's Oral History Program and get discounted admission to any of the Institute-sponsored seminars offered around the country. Discounts are also available to the colorful bimonthly magazine *Naval History.*

The Naval Institute's book-publishing program, begun in 1898 with basic guides to naval practices, has broadened its scope in recent years to include books of more general interest. Now the Naval Institute Press publishes about one hundred titles each year, ranging from how-to books on boating and navigation to battle histories, biographies, ship and aircraft guides, and novels. Institute members receive discounts of 20 to 50 percent on the Press's nearly six hundred books in print.

Full-time students are eligible for special half-price membership rates. Life memberships are also available.

For a free catalog describing Naval Institute Press books currently available, and for further information about joining the U.S. Naval Institute, please write to:

Membership Department
U.S. NAVAL INSTITUTE
291 Wood Road
Annapolis, MD 21402-5035
Telephone: (800) 233-8764
Fax: (410) 269-7940
Web address: www.usni.org